10/98

GOLF: AN ALBUM OF ITS HISTORY

GOLF:
AN ALBUM OF ITS HISTORY

Robert R. McCord

BURFORD
BOOKS

Printed in the United States of America.

10 9 8 7 6 5 4 3 2 1

Library of Congress Cataloging-in-Publication Data

McCord, Robert R.
   Golf: an album of its history / Robert R. McCord.
      p.   cm.
   Includes index.
   ISBN 1-58080-063-7 (cloth)
   1. Golf—History.   2. Golf—History—Pictorial works.   I. Title.
GV963.M33   1998
796.352'.09—dc21   98-17974
                                                            CIP

CONTENTS

DEDICATION

For Nancy, Who Played It As It Lays, With Great Warmth and Nobility

For Frank Reed McCord and His Family

ACKNOWLEDGMENTS

There are many people who have contributed to this book, directly and indirectly. First of all, I would like to thank Peter Burford, my editor and publisher, who initiated this book and saw it to its completion. Also, thanks to the photographers, photo archives, libraries and others who provided assistance on this project, most notably Marge Dewey and Saundra Sheffer at the Ralph W. Miller Golf Library, Industry City, California; Maxine Vigliotta, Patty Moran and Nancy Stulack at the United States Golf Association, Far Hills, New Jersey; Khristine Januzik at the Tufts Archives, Pinehurst, North Carolina; Rhonda Glenn, author of *The Illustrated History of Women's Golf* (Taylor Publishing, Dallas, Texas); Montana Pritchard of the PGA of America; Golfoto, Enid Oklahoma; Jim Ellis, author of *The Clubmaker's Art: Antique Clubs and Their History* (Zephyr Productions Inc., Oak Harbor, Washington); Russell Kirk; Gerald Sprayregen; Corbis-Bettman Archive, New York City; and those many golfers, writers, editors, publishers, collectors, artists, archivists and enthusiasts who have cared enough to nurture and preserve golf's rich history.

GOLF: AN ALBUM OF ITS HISTORY

INTRODUCTION

Golf: An Album of its History is a brief and eclectic pictorial stroll through the annals of this great game. Played by royals (including Mary, Queen of Scots) and commoners (like the local Saint Andrews shepherd) from its outset, golf seemed to have a universal appeal and infinite variations. Whether the game was played on ice, as it was in fourteenth-century Holland, or at some exclusive modern club, golfers have endlessly plotted and schemed to reach their target in the fewest number of strokes. The object to be struck might be a stone, wooden ball, leather-covered feather-stuffed ball, or concoction of rubber and other elements. The hitting implement might be made of wood, wood and iron, aluminum, or more elegant materials such as fiberglass and titanium. The target could be a pole, door, tree, hole, or other destination.

These earliest innocent days of golf gave way to the perceived need for a standard code of rules. The game became organized and golfing societies were formed. The first golf club is believed to have been the Honourable Company of Edinburgh Golfers, established in 1744. In order to standardize competitive rules the Royal and Ancient Golf Club at Saint Andrews adopted thirteen rules of golf in the mid-eighteenth century. This more formal game spread from Scotland to the rest of the British Isles, then to the European continent, North America, and elsewhere. Technology influenced the game, most notably in the form of the golf ball; this was first wooden, then a leather-covered sphere stuffed with wool or feathers.

The gutta-percha ball, made of sap from Malaya, began to supersede the featherie in the late 1840s. These "gutties" greatly popularized the game because they were less expensive, lasted longer, gave improved flight, and ran much truer to the green. During the first half of the nineteenth century golf clubs were typically drivers, spoons, irons, and putters. The drivers, called play clubs, were long, wooden instruments with tapering flexible shafts and small, raking heads. These clubs were generally used off the tees and on safe, grassy ground. More specialized clubs, such as the track iron used in rutted and rocky areas, had other purposes.

The interrelationships among golf ball technology, club design, the mechanics of the golf swing, golf course design, and the rules of the game provide a fascinating medley and map of the history of the sport. As golf became more popular, equipment design grew more refined. The gutta-percha ball gave way to the Haskell in the late nineteenth century; the rubber-core ball quickly became the standard. Clubs with tougher heads and stronger shafts with less torque were required to withstand the shock generated from hitting this harder ball. Makers of limited-edition clubs and balls were almost entirely replaced by manufacturers of mass-produced sets of clubs. At the same time, golf's governing bodies, the Royal and Ancient in Scotland and the United States Golf Association, began to legislate the number and types of clubs and balls that could be used in official competition.

Professional golfers, such as Allan Robertson and Tom Morris Sr. of Saint Andrews, began to emerge in the 1840s. Most reputable golf clubs had a professional who did everything from making and repairing clubs and balls to tending the greens and providing instruction. The number of holes on a golf course varied but gradually became standardized. The first national championship, the British Open, was played on the twelve-hole, 3,803-yard Prestwick course in 1860. By 1892 the British Open had become a seventy-two-hole event played on eighteen-hole layouts, such as Saint Andrews and Muirfield. Legends such as Old Tom Morris, Young Tom Morris, Harry Vardon, and others made their reputations in these tournaments and became internationally known.

The British Ladies' National Championship was inaugurated in 1893, and the Americans soon followed with the U.S. Women's Amateur in 1895. Since then many national amateur and professional events have been established, and a number or organizations, such as the National Golf Foundation, the Golf Collectors Society, the American Society of Golf Course Architects, and many regional and local golf associations, have been formed. While the rules of the game have become increasingly complex, golf participation now includes over thirty-six million people worldwide.

Golf courses themselves have evolved over time. The older courses have been remodeled and lengthened to accommodate the modern game. The introduction of a variety of hazards, ranging from wetlands and bunkers to island greens, has added to golf's challenges. Unlike the original links courses "designed by God," such as Saint Andrews, new golf courses are designed by professional golf course architects and built by construction crews with mechanized equipment. Golf course construction and maintenance techniques have become increasingly sophisticated, enabling developers to address environmental concerns and accommodate heavy daily golf traffic. Executive courses, short courses, putting courses, miniature golf, practice ranges, specially designed holes to accommodate golf schools, and other innovations have added depth and variety to the game.

We have now entered the era of multinational golf, in which the game's professional stars move from tournament to tournament in personal jet airplanes. A broad range of publications and other media document tournament results, new product introductions, and other golf events of the day. The avid golf aficionado can find stimuli on The Golf Channel, a specialized television network, the Internet, and in any number of golf videos, software, books, and magazines. The serious collector can rummage for featheries, play clubs, old golf programs, and other memorabilia.

The spirit of golf is sustained not only by its rich history but also the joy and challenge of teeing it up and trying to reach a target somewhere on the horizon, pursuits that can take place in quiet solitude or in the raucous company of good friends. The fascinating history of golf and its many enjoyable facets have intrigued golfers over time. In this book, hopefully, are some apt reminders of this tradition.

—Robert McCord
New York City, 1998

THE EARLY DAYS

SAINT ANDREWS

Overlooking the eastern shores of Scotland in the Kingdom of Fife, Saint Andrews became a golf course somewhere in the mist of time. Sheep grazing and golfing rights became the official privilege of local burghers in the 16th century. It was not until 1913 that a green fee was required on The Old Course, now a golf Mecca and mainstay in the British Open rotation. The Royal and Ancient Golf Club, arbiter of international golf rules in coordination with the United States Golf Association, is on site.

The Old Course is situated on a narrow strip of land between the old railway and the dunes along Saint Andrews Bay. The outline of the hole routing at Saint Andrews resembled a shepherd's crook. The links had twelve putting areas, ten of which served the player both on his outward trek and again on the homeward one. The arrangement led to the adoption of the terms "out" and "in" to designate which of the common holes a golfer was playing, and eventually to describe the front and back nines of a golf course. There were originally eleven holes that ran out to Eden and eleven played back home, for a total of twenty-two. In 1764 the Royal and Ancient reduced the layout to the now-standard eighteen. It was also in the eighteenth century that greens began to be specially tended at Saint Andrews for the first time. Only four holes have their own green; the others have giant double greens. This practice began in 1832 with the cutting of two cups into each of the common greens, creating the double greens on which two matches, one leading out and one heading in, could be played at once. The variable winds and numerous bunkers, such as Hell, Coffin, and Principal's Nose, make Saint Andrews an endless, frustrating mystery.

The R&A was known as the Society of Saint Andrews Golfers when it was founded May 12, 1754. In 1834 King William IV was induced to recognize the Saint Andrews Links as "Royal and Ancient." Thereafter Saint Andrews declared itself the "Home of Golf" even though the Honorable Company of Edinburgh Golfers at the Links of Leath had previously been considered the oldest club. Still, Saint Andrews became the standard by which other golf clubs and courses were measured. Between 1848 and 1850, the course was widened by replacing heather with turf and by expanding the greens into huge surfaces; it had previously severely punished the golfer who could not carry bunkers and keep the ball in play. The alterations lent a new strategic element to Saint Andrews: A golfer could take a direct route to the hole at the risk of landing in hazards, or take a longer, safer route that would likely add at least a stroke to his score.

The accompanying photo was taken at the eighteenth green during the 1926 Walker Cup matches.

BANNED IN SCOTLAND

Golf was banned in Scotland by King James II, pictured here, in 1457 because it strongly interfered with archery practice, then important for the defense of the realm against the English. Previously, in 1424, football had been forbidden by an act of the Scots Parliament under James I. Following a peace treaty between England and Scotland in 1502, the Scots were allowed to resume their golfing activities—although it remained illegal to play on Sunday. In 1553 John Hamilton, Archbishop of Saint Andrews, confirmed the communal right of playing golf over the links at the course.

When James VI of Scotland ascended the English throne in 1603 to become James I of England, he introduced golf to that country. It is believed that royally endorsed golf was first played on Blackheath Common in 1608, but the game did not at first appeal to the English. The Royal Blackheath Golf Club, however, did come into existence in 1766, and golf has since then become a favorite pastime of the English.

EARLY LADY GOLFERS: MARY, QUEEN OF SCOTS

Mary, Queen of Scots, pictured here, was one of the earliest notable woman golfers. Her decision to play a round in the fields of Seton House in 1567 shortly after the death of her husband, Lord Darnley, contributed to her downfall. The first women's golf tournament was organized in Musselburgh in 1811 for the town's "fishwives." The first ladies' club, the Saint Andrews Ladies', was formed in 1867. The Ladies' Golf Union was established in Britain in 1893, as was the Ladies' Championship. Separate women's golf courses became a rarity as women gradually were allowed to play at men's clubs. The first workable golf handicapping system was developed by the Ladies' Golf Union and later adopted by the men.

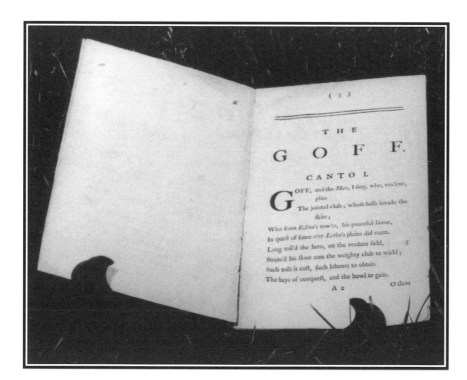

THE FIRST GOLF BOOK

The Goff, by Thomas Mathison, published in 1743, is considered the first book whose single subject was golf. The full title of this twenty-two-page classic is *The Goff: A Heroi-Comical Poem in Three Cantos.* Earlier references to the game of golf include the Acts of Parliament, written in 1457. The earliest printed reference to English golf has been found in *Instructions to a Son*, written by the Marques of Argyle and published in England in 1689. Some collectors argue that a small volume of poetry, entitled *Glotta*, and written by James Arbuckle, a student at Glasgow University circa 1721, was the first important contribution to golf literature. The first appearance in North America of information on the game is found in "Sermons to Gentlemen upon Temperance and Exercise," a pamphlet written by Dr. Benjamin Rush of Philadelphia and printed in 1722. Among its droll observations on the value of golf are: "The late Dr. M'Kenzie, Author of the effay on Health and Long Life, ufed to fay, that a man would live ten years longer for ufing this exercise once or twice a week."

WINTER SCENE WITH FIGURES PLAYING KOLF

There is debate as to whether the Dutch created a forerunner of modern golf, refined by the Scots, or whether it just resembled an already extant Scottish game. The Dutch game was kolfspel, so called because it was played with a club (kolf, plural kloven in Dutch; the verb kloven means "to play kolfspel"). Dutch historian Steven Van Hengel claims that a version of golf was played in the village of Loenen aan de Vecht as early as 1297. The game has been traced to numerous other Dutch cities as early as the 1400s. The Dutch version of golf could be played on ice, usually toward a post, or on grass where a hole was the target. Wooden as well as leather tennis balls were used during this period. Van Hengel estimates that leather balls, also used for hand tennis, were produced at the rate of 500,000 per year during the 16th century. The oceangoing Dutch exported many of these to Scotland and there is evidence that sometimes the crew took their clubs with them.

Many of the clues to early Dutch golf come from paintings and illustrations of outdoor life in the Netherlands. Early Dutch painters show several forms of kolfspel, particularly the version played on ice. Depicted here is "Winter Scene With Figures Playing Kolf" by Aert van der Neer, a Dutch artist who lived from 1603-1677.

LINKS COURSES

The earliest courses along the coastline of Scotland were known as links because they linked the arable land to the sea. Wind and water shaped the dunes, knolls, ridges, and hollows that proved ideal terrain for golf. Gorse, heather, and broom provided tenacious rough. Fescue, marron, bent, and meadow grasses springing from sandy soil added variety, beauty, and mystery to the game. Natural bunkers were often gaping chasms that might occasionally shelter an animal. On these venues the early style of play was to perfect run-up shots to firm greens, which would not hold lofted shots. Low shots took the wind out of play, and hooked shots sometimes seemed to roll forever on fairways without sprinkler systems. Pictured here is the old course at Troon, Scotland, a traditional links course.

THE RULES OF GOLF

The rules of golf appear to be simple, given that the object of the game, according to modern Rule 1, is "in playing the ball from the teeing ground into the hole by successive strokes in accordance with The Rules." The original rules were a code of thirteen drawn up in 1744 by the Honorable Company of Edinburgh Golfers in order to standardize competitions. (Before that, individual clubs generally conducted match-play competitions and resolved disputes among themselves; the rules could vary from club to club.) In 1754 the Royal and Ancient Golf Club at Saint Andrews adopted the Leith Rules, reprinted below. In 1759 the practice of keeping score by strokes, rather than by holes, was introduced.

With the development of the gutta-percha ball in the late 1840s, along with the increased accessibility of golf and the demand for more competition, there also came a need to have a body governing the sport's rules. In 1888 the R&A drew up a code, including a separate section for its own particular rules; by 1897 the R&A had become generally accepted as golf's ruling body. However, disputes over the rules continued. The USGA, established in 1894, began adding to the R&A code. Disputes over equipment standards, format of play (match play versus medal, for instance), and other issues arose.

Finally, a uniform code was agreed upon by the R&A and the USGA in 1952. The R&A, for example, agreed to allow the center-shafted putter—which it had outlawed after American Walter Travis won the British Amateur with it in 1904-back into the game. Representatives of the R&A and the USGA now meet at regular intervals to codify the game and coordinate its rules.

ARTICLES AND LAWS IN PLAYING THE GOLF
(MAY 14, 1754)

You must tee your ball within a club-length of the hole.

Your tee must be upon the ground.

You are not to change the ball which you strike off the tee.

You are not to remove stones, bones or any break-club for the sake of playing your ball, except upon the fair green, and that only within a club length of your ball.

If your ball come among water or any watery filth, you are at liberty to take your ball and throw it behind the hazard six yards at least; you may play it with any club, and allow your adversary a stroke for so getting out your ball.

If your balls be found anywhere touching one another, you are to lift the first ball until you play the last.

At holing you are to play your ball honestly for the hole, and not to play upon your adversary's ball, not lying in your way to the hole.

If you should lose your ball by its being taken up or any other way, you are to go back to the spot where you struck last and drop another ball and allow you adversary a stroke for the misfortune.

No man at holing his ball is to be allowed to mark his way to the hole with his club or anything else.

If a ball is stop'd by any person, horse, dog or anything else, the ball so stop'd must be played where it lyes.

If you draw your club in order to strike and proceed so far with your stroke as to be bringing down your club, if then your club should break in any way, it is accounted as a stroke.

He whose ball lyes furthest from the hole is obliged to play first.

Neither trench, ditch, or dyke made for the preservation of the links, nor the Scholars' Holes, nor the Soldiers Lines, shall be accounted a hazard, but the ball is to be taken out, teed, and played with any iron club.

The First
Professionals

THE FIRST PROFESSIONALS

Allan Robertson (1815–1859) was born in Saint Andrews and was considered the best golfer of the first half of the nineteenth century—until Tom Morris Sr., his golfing partner and protégé in the ball- and club-making business, came along. Robertson was the first notable golf professional and was said never to have lost a singles match-play contest of any significance. It was Robertson's strategy to win his matches by small margins in order to increase the bet or the odds for his next match. Tom Morris once described him as "an awfu player with the conningest bit body of a player that ever handled club, cleek or putter." At the time of his death in September 1859, the *Dundee Advertiser* newspaper called him "the first of Champions" and claimed: "Allan Robertson, the greatest golf-player that ever lived, of whom alone in the annals of the pastime it can be said that he never was beaten, was born in St. Andrews on the 11th of September 1815. . . . It is a fact that his playthings as a child were golf clubs."

One of Robertson's most notable victories was a match-play win over Willie Dunn in a twenty-round, 360-hole contest in 1843. Among Robertson's strategic contributions to the game was his introduction of iron rather than wooden play clubs for approach shots to the green.

OLD TOM MORRIS: A SAINT ANDREWS LEGEND

Old Tom Morris, born in Saint Andrews in 1821, was one of the pioneers of professional golf. Old Tom won the British Open four times (1861, 1862, 1864, 1867), thereby gaining an international reputation as one of the best in the game. Morris was a club- and ball-maker and junior partner of Allan Robertson in Saint Andrews. The two often teamed up in match-play events to defeat competitors such as Willie and Jamie Dunn of Musselburgh. In a famous high-stakes (four hundred pounds) match over Musselburgh, Saint Andrews, and North Berwick in 1849, the Dunns were up four holes with eight to play in the final round at North Berwick. Morris and Robertson caught them on the sixteenth, however, and won the match. Robertson and Morris had a business falling-out because Morris favored the new gutta-percha ball, while his partner wished to continue with the traditional featherie. Tom moved from Saint Andrews to Prestwick, site of the first British Open in 1860, where he became custodian of the links. He later returned to Saint Andrews, though, where he served as green-keeper until 1904. He operated a club-making and ball-making shop beside the eighteenth green. His portrait hangs in the nearby Royal and Ancient clubhouse.

YOUNG TOM MORRIS: THE MAN WHO RETIRED THE BRITISH OPEN CHAMPIONSHIP BELT

Young Tom Morris, (at right, with his father "Old Tom") born in Saint Andrews in 1851, is the only player to have retired the British Open Championship belt, a result of consecutive wins in 1868, 1869, and 1870. The tournament was not held in 1871; then Tom won it again in 1872 to become the only man to win four consecutive Opens. Young Tom joined his father, a four-time British Open champion, to form a deadly match-play team. In September 1875 the two defeated Willie and Mungo Park in a famous match at North Berwick.

After that contest Young Tom was advised that his wife and child were seriously ill back in Saint Andrews. He traveled by boat to reach them but they both passed away before his arrival. Tom died shortly thereafter, at age twenty-four, on Christmas Day, 1875. The inscription on the memorial at his resting place in Saint Andrews Cathedral reads: "Deeply regretted by numerous friends and all golfers, he thrice in succession won the championship belt and held it without rivalry and yet without envy, his many amiable qualities being no less acknowledged than his golfing achievements."

THE CADDIE: A GOLFER'S FRIEND AND CRITIC

The caddie traditionally is a person skilled in the game who, for a fee, carries clubs and offers advice. The word *caddie* is a Scottish form of the French word *cadet*. The term can be traced to younger sons of French noble families who went to Edinburgh in the entourage of Mary, Queen of Scots, an avid golfer. Alister Mackenzie, the noted Scottish golf course architect, commented on Saint Andrews caddies: "Even the Saint Andrews caddies are quite different to anywhere else. Their knowledge and advice on the course makes them look on themselves as the principal partners in the match. In describing a match they use the personal pronoun 'I', not even 'We', and say, 'I skelped an iron on to the first green', and so on." Pictured here is Fiery, a noted Musselburgh caddie, who died in 1913.

SCOTTISH GOLF AMBASSADORS

The Dutch are sometimes credited with originating golf, although the Scottish later made the game their own. Written records date back as far as 1353 of a cross-country version of golf in Holland with four players to a side. The objective was to strike the doors of selected buildings along the way with a wooden ball, the equivalent of "holing out." The victors generally won a barrel of beer. Thus, perhaps, began the tradition of the nineteenth hole. The Dutch provided the Scots with their featherie golf balls until the Scottish king decided to promote domestic production. Early Scottish port towns, such as Saint Andrews, Musselburgh, and Dornoch traded with the Dutch.

Games similar to golf were also played by the Romans, French, Belgians, Germans, and Chinese. But the Scots perfected it and sent emissaries, who promoted the game to the rest of the world. Old Willie Dunn, pictured here, was the first Scottish professional golfer to leave his homeland to promote golf. He went to Blackheath, outside London in 1851. By 1888 there were seventy-three golf courses in Scotland, fifty-seven in England, six in Ireland and two in Wales.

BOB FERGUSON: THREE-TIME WINNER OF THE BRITISH OPEN

Bob Ferguson (1848–1915) of Musselburgh entered golf history by winning the British Open three consecutive times (1880, 1881, 1882), as had Young Tom Morris (1868, 1869, 1870, 1872), Jamie Anderson of Saint Andrews, a quick player who was noted for his accurate approach shots and who was also a fine club maker (1877, 1878, 1879), and, later, Peter Thomson (1954, 1955, 1956). Ferguson, who began as a caddie at Musselburgh at the age of eight, became an acknowledged money player when he defeated a group of professionals at a tournament in Leith at eighteen. His prize money was ten pounds sterling. Thereafter he was backed by various sponsors, including Sir Charles Tennant, who put up money in 1868 and 1869 when Ferguson beat Tom Morris in six matches. A strong man, Ferguson was known for his excellent long-iron play.

Ferguson almost became the second person, after Young Tom Morris, to win four consecutive British Opens, but he lost at Musselburgh in 1883 after tying Willie Fernie, then a professional at Dumfries. During the regular rounds, Fernie had a 10 on one hole but finished with an aggregate score of 159 for thirty-six holes of play—the only British Open champion to have had a double-figure score on one hole. Still, in the playoff, then an eighteen-hole stroke-play affair, Ferguson led by a stroke going into the last hole, a par 4, but Fernie eagled the eighteenth to win the championship.

WILLIE PARK: WINNER OF THE FIRST BRITISH OPEN

Willie Park Sr. was a member of a renowned Scottish golfing family long associated with Musselburgh. Park was the first winner of the British Open, in 1860, and later won three more (1863, 1866, 1873). His 1860 Open victory was against a field of eight golfers. The event was comprised of three rounds of golf over the twelve-hole Prestwick, Scotland, course—the sole site of the Open until it was played at Saint Andrews in 1873. Park shot a 174 in that first thirty-six-hole event. His archrival, Tom Morris Sr., finished second with a score of 176. Park finished second four times in the Open, which is now rotated among courses at Royal Saint George's, Royal Birkdale, Royal Lytham, and Saint Annes in England; and Saint Andrews, Turnberry, Royal Troon, and Muirfield in Scotland.

The first British national championships (interclub foursomes) were initiated by a letter sent out in 1857 by the Prestwick Club to seven other clubs: Saint Andrews, Perth, Musselburgh, Blackheath, Prestwick, Carnoustie, North Berwick, and Leven. These clubs were invited to play an amateur championship, and they all accepted. Four other clubs also participated in the event, which was won by Royal Blackheath in a final against Saint Andrews, where the event was held. All of the match-play contests were played out even if one team had closed out the match; both contestants in a halved match advanced to the next round. This first event was played by foursomes from each club. The following year it became an individual match-play competition, much like the current British Amateur. The first official British Amateur was played at the Royal Liverpool Club at Hoylake in 1885 and won by A. F. MacFie of Royal Liverpool.

WILLIE PARK JR.: THE FIRST PROFESSIONAL TO AUTHOR A BOOK

Willie Park Jr. (1864–1925) was the son of the three-time British Open winner and the nephew of Mungo Park, winner of the 1874 Open. Willie Jr. won the Open in 1887 and 1889. He engaged in high-stakes match play against Andrew Kirkaldy, J. H. Taylor, Harry Vardon, and other heavy hitters of his era. Putting was a major strength of his game, but big hitters such as Vardon were difficult for him to defeat. Along with his relatives, Park was among the early golf course architects. He designed and remodeled numerous golf courses in Europe and North America, including the Olympia Field North Course in Illinois (1923) and the Sunningdale Golf Club Old Course in England (1901). He also was an entrepreneur and businessman, a club-maker, inventor, and author. He wrote *The Game of Golf* (1896)—the first book authored by a professional golfer—and *The Art of Putting* (1920).

GOLF EQUIPMENT
AND TECHNIQUE

EARLY GOLF BALLS: THE FEATHERIE ERA

The golf ball can be traced to the 1400s, when it is believed wooden balls were used. The featherie ball, a leather-encased sphere stuffed with goose down or chicken feathers, is believed to have originated in the seventeenth century. The wet leather, usually $5/32$-inch-thick bull or horsehide, would shrink, as would the feathers, to form a rather hard ball. Because these balls took around three hours to make and were thus expensive, the upper classes generally were the predominant golfers until the 1840s. At that point gutta-perchas, made from rubberlike material from the dried sap of sapodilla trees of East Asia, came into use.

A feather ball's playability varied depending on its size or weight; the latter ranged from around 1.32 to 1.82 ounces (today's ball weighs a standard 1.62 ounces and is 1.62 inches in circumference). Feather ball players selected balls based on their skill level, the lay of the course, and the day's playing conditions. The typical featherie was not always perfectly round, but tended toward an oblong shape. And it seldom lasted more than a day.

In a letter dated August 5, 1618, James I granted James Melvill a twenty-one-year monopoly to manufacture featheries, ostensibly to develop a local golf ball industry and reduce dependence on Dutch-manufactured balls. In fact Melvill obtained a license and subcontracted the manufacture of balls to others. Historians have traced the first featheries shipped to the United States to the Dear family of Charleston, South Carolina, who reportedly received three gross (432) balls on May 10, 1743. Pictured here is a featherie ball.

EARLY GOLF CLUBS

In the beginning golfers were content to use one club for all shots. But by the end of the fifteenth century there were clubs for specific purposes. Shots from the tee, and many through the green where the lies were good, were made with the play club, the forerunner of the driver. And there were other wooden clubs with greater angles of loft, which were used from doubtful lies or in approach play where the ball had to be given more loft.

The earliest iron clubs were few in number and were used specifically for playing out of bunkers and rough places. These had names like bunker iron and track iron. All approach play from reasonable lies was with lofted wooden clubs—the long spoon, short spoon, baffing spoon (baffy) and others. Depicted here are, from the left, a mid-spoon made by Old Tom Morris; a play club by James McEwan; a brassie by Willie Park Jr.; a play club by Robert Forgan, the Prince of Wales's club maker; and a play club by Hugh Philp. Philp (1782–1852) is considered the Stradivarius of club makers. Fewer than two hundred of his elegant masterpieces are known to exist.

THE GUTTA-PERCHA: THE BALL AND THE GAME EVOLVE

The gutta-percha ball replaced the comparatively expensive featherie ball in the late 1840s and lasted into the twentieth century. The earliest gutta-percha balls were formed from pieces of gutta-percha and rounded by hand. Molds were later used, and six dozen or more gutty balls could be produced in a day by a skilled ball maker—as opposed to three by a featherie maker. The Reverend James Paterson of Dundee is credited with making the first gutty in 1845. At the outset, the balls were smooth and traveled erratically like a Whiffle Ball. Dimples were added to improve the aerodynamics, and a variety of intricate patterns were devised including circles, triangles, letters, commas, and other exotic designs. Willie Dunn created a "Stars and Stripes" flag-patterned ball, which is now eagerly sought by collectors. The gutta-perchas were hand hammered with patterns until around 1880, when the use of molds superseded the hammering process.

The hardness of the gutty often did damage to wooden-faced golf clubs of the time, making necessary the use of leather or fiber inserts in the club face. In warm weather the gutty softened and did not carry as far; in cold weather it became brittle and could actually break up upon contact. A rules change resulted, allowing the golfer to drop a new ball near the largest remaining piece of a gutty ball .

Gutty balls were painted and required repainting after use. A remade market developed in which old gutties were retooled, repainted, and resold at a discount. Collectors favor a gutty that had little play and was not remade. Pictured here is a nineteenth-century gutta-percha ball factory in Great Britain before the era of machine-made balls.

GOLF ATTIRE

In the late 1800s when golf was being popularized by the gutta-percha, the development of golf clubs, and regular formal competitions, gentlemen often played in a coat and tie, and ladies in cumbersome attire such as long dresses, corsets, and other unmentionables. The men's attire was usually similar to that used in other outdoor pursuits, such as fishing and shooting. The women's attire was much more penal. A typical nineteenth-century lady's outfit might have been comprised of red coats with buttons of gilt bearing the club crest, medals on the left breast in military style, deep starched collars, a belt with broad webbing and a huge buckle with club insignia or the owner's monograms, voluminous cloth or tweed skirts, and thick boots fastened with metal tackets. On the golfer's head was usually a stiff boater with braids of club colors around the crowns.

As golf became more democratized and as fashion evolved, more comfortable casual wear prevailed. Yet Babe Didrikson Zaharias was asked to change out of her red, white, and blue checked shorts at the British Ladies' in 1947. She wore a skirt and won anyway. Shown here is a threesome of ladies preparing to play in Clifton, Massachusetts, in 1898.

THE PALM GRIP

With the advent of the gutta-percha ball, golf club grips became larger, because the harder ball generated shock up the club shaft into the hands. The larger grips with wool under-lasting required larger hands and the grasping of the club more in the palms than in the fingers. As a result the palm grip, demonstrated here by S. Mure Fergusson, winner of the Royal and Ancient Gold Medal in 1913, was commonly used during the last half of the nineteenth century, before Haskell and rubber-core balls became commonplace. The palm grip entailed grasping the club with both hands separately, with both thumbs around the club shaft. The torque or whippiness in shafts was reduced by making them of hickory which allowed the player to hit rather than sweep the ball from the tee. A more compact club head was developed, too, to improve upon the long-nosed splice head.

THE UPRIGHT SWING

The gutta-percha ball made it difficult for a player using traditional clubs and the standard stance to get adequate loft on the ball. Players found that if they moved closer to the ball and adopted an upright swing stance, the ball would fly higher. This more upright swing was facilitated by shorter clubs. The newer clubs, such as the Vardon wood of the 1890s, were approximately three inches shorter than the traditional play clubs of the featherie era.

Players such as Harry Vardon and James Braid adopted an open stance to go with the new upright stance and shorter clubs, enabling them to get the ball up in the air. The Vardon swing was adopted as the model swing at the turn of the century. Because of bulky clothing worn by most players, a bent left arm was typical at the top of the swing. Backswings became shorter, and the hands and forearms tended to be used for power.

By the end of the nineteenth century in Britain you could generally recognize a player's home region by his swing. The Saint Andrews swing was long and flowing. Hoylake was an open stance with the ball toward the right foot. North Berwick's stance had the ball played forward. Equipment changes—the advent of Haskell and rubber-core balls, steel shafts, hickory shafts, shorter clubs, and drop forged-iron heads—led to even further experimentation with the setup and swing. Pictured here, Bobby Jones and his upright swing.

THE STYMIE

The stymie is a situation in match play on the putting green in which one side's ball blocks the line of the other side's ball to the hole and the latter must attempt to play past, around, or over the blocking ball. The stymie was abolished in 1951.

THE GREEN

The putting green, of course, has a hole cut in the ground; it is the object of the golfer to advance the ball into this hole in as few strokes as possible. In the old days greens were sandy seaside linksland surfaces on natural terrain not specially tended. Saint Andrews didn't carefully tend its greens until into the twentieth century. Most of its putting surfaces are huge double greens, whereas Troon in Ayrshire, Scotland, features the famous small "Postage Stamp" green at its eighth hole, a par 3. The term *green-keeper* refers to someone who maintains the entire course, not just the greens. This stems from a longer tradition of having no greens to speak of.

There is no limit to the size or contour of a green. As any golfer knows, some are relatively flat, others have subtle undulations, and still others might have pronounced slopes or a variety of shelves. The Stimpmeter provides a measure of green speed. The higher the number, the faster the speed. The Masters at Augusta National features fast greens at tournament time—around 13 on the Stimpmeter. The average resort golf course usually has moderately fast greens—in the 7 or 8 Stimpmeter range. Augusta National is a traditional parkland course cut from a scenic arboretum. It has pronounced elevation changes, strategically placed trees, water hazards, and a collection of bunkers guarding the greens. But the course has no rough and measures around seven thousand yards from the championship tees, so green speed and difficult pin placements are used to keep the professionals from dominating the golf course at tournament time.

All in all manicured greens have become part of carefully tended courses that are quite different from the old seaside links, where you had to contend with wind, gorse, bunkers and such other obstacles as farm animals and the people who also strolled this common ground.

Pictured here is a sand putting green at Pinehurst, North Carolina, in the early 1900s.

THE HASKELL BALL: NEW TECHNOLOGY REPLACES THE GUTTY

The Haskell ball, patented by Coburn Haskell in 1898, was a three-piece ball: Its center core was wound around with a rubber thread then covered with a molded gutta-percha material. After a few years of experimentation, the cores became larger and the covers thinner, as this combination provided truer flight. The refined Haskell proved much more forgiving than gutta-percha. It flew higher, shocked less when mishit, and traveled twenty-five to thirty yards farther. Initially the balls were constructed by hand winding elastic thread around a rubber core under great tension. In 1900 John Gammeter invented and patented automatic winding machinery that allowed the rubber ball to be economically mass-produced.

The early Haskells were called "Bounding Billys," because they tended to duck and dart when they landed. A notable modification was the 1907 introduction of the dimple pattern, which helped players control ball trajectories and aerodynamic spin. Yet the die was cast in favor of the Haskell when Walter Travis won the U.S. Amateur with it in 1901. Driving distance for a Haskell was in the 210- to 270-yard range; the average distance was around 240 yards. The driving distance for a gutty, on the other hand, was reportedly in the 170- to 190-yard range, and the featherie averaged around 150 yards off the tee. Yet for every generalization there are exceptions. It is recorded that in 1836, Monsieur Samuel Messieux, winner of the Royal and Ancient Gold Medal in 1827, hit a featherie 361 yards under ideal conditions, over icy elysian fields on a frosty day. Many argue that featheries indeed traveled farther than gutties, but were expensive and easily became misshapen. Courses were lengthened and made more penal in order to offset advances in golf ball and club technology.

The Haskell compressed more than its predecessors, stayed on the club face longer when struck, and generated more height and backspin. Wooden clubs were then manufactured with more club face depth to avoid the skied shots generated by traditional shallower clubs. Allan Robertson's play club of the 1840s was only $^{15}/_{16}$-inch in depth. A typical club at the turn of the century was about $1^{3}/_{16}$-inches and today's woods can be over 3 inches in depth.

On January 1, 1931, the USGA ruled that no ball could be played in championships that weighed more than 1.55 ounces or was smaller in diameter than 1.68 inches. The Royal and Ancient and the USGA eventually worked out a compromise on weight and size standards. The R&A fixed the official weight and size at a maximum of 1.62 ounces and a minimum of 1.62 inches. The USGA sanctioned the 1.62-ounce maximum weight but maintained 1.68 inches as the minimum diameter.

THE PUTTER

In the first half of the nineteenth century there were generally two types of putters: driving putters, for approach shots over unencumbered terrain, and green putters, for use on the putting green. The golf historian Robert Browning believes that the word *putt* was originally used in golf in much the same way as *putting the weight* in other sports. Any shot intended to keep the ball low was deemed a putt. In the days of the featherie, greens were rough ground and the notion of rolling a ball in with a putter was not common, because the ball could not be trusted to roll straight. It was only as greens became more manicured and the ball more reliably round that modern putting became the norm.

The biggest putter controversy occurred when Walter Travis, an Australian-born American golfer, decided to use a center-shafted Schenectady putter in the 1904 British Amateur. The club, whose shaft was inserted into a mallet-shaped head, was called a Schenectady because it had been invented by a resident of that city, A. W. Knight. Travis won the Amateur with his Schenectady and the R&A, affronted by the new technology, banned the club until the early 1950s. The Schenectady putter shown here is the only known model made of cast iron. The standard model was made of lightweight aluminum.

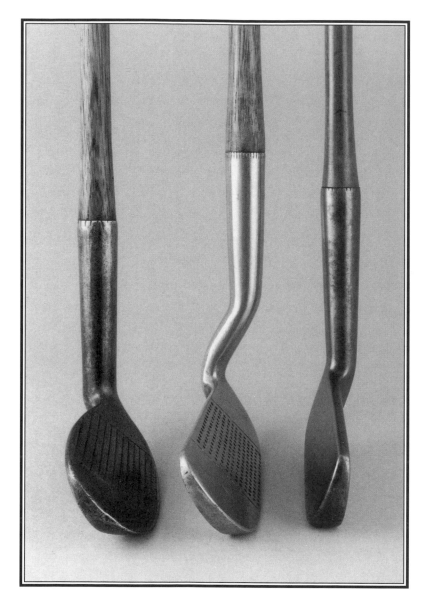

FORGED-IRON CLUBS

Club making has become a science as well as a vigorous marketing game. Club makers who evolved from craft guilds, such as those formed by bow makers and furniture makers, have become extinct, as have the colorful names and configurations assigned to mid-19th- and early 20th-century clubs. Before 1850 a typical set of golf clubs was comprised of woods—a play club (driver), a variety of wooden spoons (long spoon, short spoon, mid-spoon, baffing spoon), plus a wooden putter. A well-equipped golfer might also have a small-headed track iron for getting the ball out of wagon ruts or animal tracks, and another large-faced, less lofted iron for scraping the ball from tight lies. The shafts of the early clubs were made of hazel and later of ash. Both tended to be very whippy. To minimize torque, which was difficult to control, the ball was swept from the tee more with a body-and-arm motion than with the hands.

One important change in club design resulting from the introduction of the gutty was that splicing head and shaft together was abandoned in favor of inserting the end of the shaft into a hole in the club head. Another major innovation was the use of forged-iron clubs for approach play. Pictured here are forged irons with varying lofts and hickory shafts. At the turn of the twentieth century, typical irons included the "cleek," a shallow-faced hickory-shafted iron—then the longest of all iron clubs—with a loft roughly corre-

sponding to the modern No. 2 iron. Another iron club made popular by golfers like J.H. Taylor was the "mashie," a compromise between a lofted iron and the "niblick," whose head was round, small and heavy, and which was used to extricate balls from bad lies. The "mid-iron" was similar to a modern day 5-iron, and was typically used for distance and loft when approaching the green.

The number of clubs golfers could carry was restricted to fourteen in 1938; prior to that they could carry as many as they wanted. In the old days a golfer carried a few clubs without a bag while hitting a featherie ball around a links course that ranged from just a few to as many as twenty-two. Chick Evans carried only seven clubs when he won the 1916 U.S. Open. Clubs are now numbered and woods have the degree of loft indicated on the head.

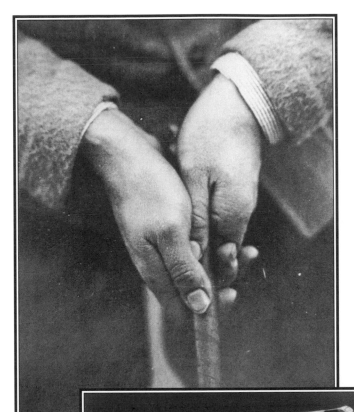

THE VARDON GRIP

Balata is a hard, resilient substance derived from the gum of the bully or balata tree of northeastern South America and the West Indies. Used as cover material, it created a softer feel on the club face which permitted the padding under the grips to be reduced; this in turn allowed the reduction of the grip's size. The grip could then be controlled more by the fingers and the Vardon overlapping grip—actually first used by golfers other than Harry Vardon—became standard. In it, the hands were rotated toward the thumbs, which favored a stronger left-hand position, showing three knuckles. Vardon taught that the gripping emphasis should be between the thumb and finger of each hand, claiming that these were the control centers.

Variations of the golf grip were often decided by the size of a player's hands. Traditionally the club grip has been covered by leather or rubber to prevent the club from slipping. The position of the hands, and other factors, govern whether the club will be square at impact. Vardon overlapping, interlocking, and other grips have been attempted.

Tommy Armour, the noted golf professional, claimed, "The basic factor in all good golf is the grip. Get it right and other progress follows."

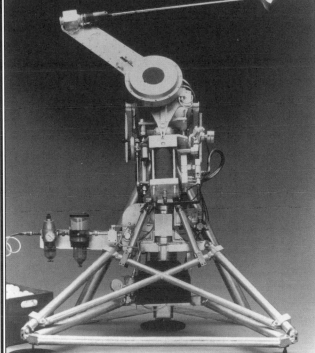

IRON BYRON

In 1941 the USGA developed a machine to test the initial velocity of balls. The machine was designed to mimic the exceptionally smooth swing of pro Byron Nelson, and is still in use today. In 1942 the USGA set the velocity limit of a ball struck by the Iron Byron at 250 feet per second (plus or minus $2\frac{1}{2}$ percent) at seventy degrees Fahrenheit, at sea level. This ruling standardized the driving distance specifications of balls and left ball manufacturers only looking for ways to improve durability and the playing life of the ball. Pictured here is an early version of the Iron Byron.

TURF MAINTENANCE

Since the late 1800s greenkeepers have been experimenting with different grasses and with methods for maintaining turf. Seedsman Martin H. Sutton, a pioneer in grass studies for golf courses, established Sutton's Grass Station in 1863 at Reading, England. By 1910 the practice of mowing fairways by using horses with leather boots pulling single mowers became common in America. In 1914 Charles Worthington introduced a horse-drawn three-unit mower, and in 1919 built a golf course tractor. By the end of World War I the use of multibladed steel mowers on greens was universal. In 1917 C. V. Piper and R.A. Oakley published *Turf for Golf Courses*, the first American book devoted to the subject. In 1920 the Green Section of the United States Golf Association was established to advise on turf problems of member courses. In the 1930s Pennsylvania State University established a turf grass extension and research team. Today a variety of universities and organizations provide research and other support for developing and maintaining golf courses. Pictured here is golf course maintenance the old-fashioned way, around the turn of the century.

THE TEE

Somewhere back in time it was decided that the first shot on each hole could be teed up. *Tee* originally meant the teeing ground, not the implement used to support the ball. By the eighteenth century bags of sand were carried to serve as teeing material, and eventually trays or boxes of sand were placed around teeing areas. Many teeing theories ensued. Harry Vardon opined, "The ball should be perched on the sand so that none of the latter can be seen; the ball should seem to be sitting clear of the ground, supported by nothing." A turn-of-the-century golf book shows a nicely-formed sand tee, at left.

By the end of the nineteenth century, the sand tee grew to be considered messy and inconsistent, and golfers began to develop individual portable gadgets that would serve as tees. Most tended to lie flat on the ground.

W. Bloxsom and A. Douglas of Scotland received the first tee patent worldwide in 1889. The first in America was filed for on December 16, 1895, by Prosper L. Senat of Philadelphia. His was a paper or cardboard annulus-shaped device that combined the raising of the ball from the ground with a means of keeping score (the paper tee could be used as a scorecard). A number of other tee devices—paper, cardboard, tethered, weighted rubber, metal, and more—have since been developed.

George F. Grant, a Boston dentist, patented the wooden golf tee, similar to the one commonly used today, in 1899. Another dentist, Dr. William Lowell of New Jersey, patented a wooden peg tee in 1924 but could not protect his patent in court cases, most notably a 1932 U.S. Circuit Court of Appeals case presided over by Judge Learned Hand. Lowell's patent was considered a "restraint of trade" during those difficult economic times. Lowell's company, Nieblo Manufacturing, was insolvent by 1933, the heart of the Great Depression. More competitors entered the market, including plastic tee manufacturers, and today, tees are a commodity item.

EARLY 20TH CENTURY
EUROPEAN GOLF

THE TRIUMVERATE: VARDON, TAYLOR, AND BRAID

Harry Vardon (1870–1937), a native of Grouville, Jersey, of the British Channel Islands, became known as one of the "Great Triumverate," along with James Braid and J. H. Taylor. This threesome asserted British international golf supremacy until the Americans emerged after World War I. Vardon won the British Open a record six times, and won the U.S. Open in 1900. Not only did he raise the level of the game of golf through his consistent championship play, but he also influenced the mechanics of the game through his overlapping Vardon grip and upright stance. Unlike most other golfers of his day, he allowed his left arm to bend, although he straightened it through his graceful downswing. He used shorter, lighter clubs than most golfers of his era. And though only five feet, five inches in height, Vardon was noted for his length off the tee.

Vardon made a major contribution to American golf with his visit to the United States in 1900 in a national tour promoting golf through a series of exhibitions. Vardon was also one of the earliest golf equipment endorsers when he promoted the Vardon Flyer, a gutta-percha ball for Spalding.

J. H. TAYLOR: WINNER OF FIVE BRITISH OPENS

J. H. Taylor, born in Northam, Devon, England, in 1871, was a member of the great British golf triumverate along with James Braid and Harry Vardon. Taylor's compact swing from a firm-footed stance was well suited to the unpredictable conditions of British golf. A fierce competitor, he often partnered with Braid or Vardon in big match-play money events. He won the British Open five times (1894, 1895, 1900, 1909, 1913) and was runner-up five times. In 1894 the British Open was held on an English course—Royal Saint George's club at Sandwich—for the first time, and Taylor's victory marked the first time an English professional had won that event. Taylor was instrumental in founding the British PGA, which helped to raise the status and enhance the livelihood of golf professionals in Great Britain. Although he left school at the age of eleven, he was well read and wrote *Golf, My Life's Work* as testimony to his love of the game.

JAMES BRAID: FIRST MAN TO WIN THE BRITISH OPEN FIVE TIMES

James Braid (1870–1950) was the son of a ploughman in Fife, Scotland. He left school at age thirteen and ten years later became a golf professional. He was the first man to win the British Open five times—although J. H. Taylor, Harry Vardon, Peter Thomson, and Tom Watson later equaled or surpassed that mark. There were few professional championships in Braid's day, so he earned a living playing challenge matches and serving as a professional at Walton Heath. In 1950 Braid, Taylor, and Willie Auchterlonie were elected honorary members of the Royal and Ancient Golf Club at Saint Andrews, the first professionals to receive that distinction.

JOHN BALL: FIRST AMATEUR TO WIN THE BRITISH OPEN

John Ball, born in Hoylake, Cheshire, England, in 1882, was the son of the owner of the Royal Hotel near the site of the Liverpool Hunt Club racecourse, which served as the Royal Liverpool Golf Club's first headquarters. Ball took up the game of golf at a young age and finished sixth in the British Open at age fifteen. One of the greatest amateur golfers of all time, Ball won the British Amateur eight times and the 1890 British Open. He was the first amateur and first Englishman to win the Open.

During the "Golden Age" of the British Amateur (1887–1895) rivals John Ball and John Laidlay won the title six times between them. Ball's style was a bit unorthodox: He used the palm grip with both hands well under the club shaft. He used an exaggeratedly open stance but had a smooth swing and an even temper for the game.

Bernard Darwin (1876–1961) was an early pioneer of golf journalism. The grandson of Charles Darwin, the great naturalist, he served as a scribe for *The Times* and *Country Life* and was a noted essayist. Darwin was also a highly intelligent, capable amateur golfer. He captained the Cambridge University golf team, practiced law, then turned to writing in 1907. In 1922 he played in the first Walker Cup tournament and was captain of the Royal and Ancient Golf Club. Among his noteworthy golf books are *Golf Between Two Wars*, *Out of the Rough*, and his autobiography, *The World That Fred Made*.

Another Cambridge graduate who added to British golf letters is Henry Longhurst, born in Bedfordshire, England, in 1909 and later captain of the golf team at Cambridge. Longhurst was a pioneer golf broadcaster and was a regular columnist for the *Evening Standard*. He also authored and coauthored several books on golf, including *It Was Good While It Lasted*, *Golf Mixture*, and various golf travel books.

LADY MARGARET SCOTT: EARLY LADY SUPERSTAR

Lady Margaret Scott was among golf's earliest stars. Born in 1873, she was the winner of the first three British Ladies' Championships (1893, 1894, 1895). Enid Wilson, an excellent golfer and later a golf journalist, observed, "Lady Margaret must have been exceptionally supple, because we have pictures of her swinging with the club almost past the ball at the top of her backswing—a horrible sight to modern teachers. On this tremendous backswing, her left heel hardly moved from the ground, and this is all the more remarkable when we consider the fashions of the 1890s, which demanded tight lacing and wasp waists." Scott retired undefeated after her third victory and became Lady Margaret Hamilton-Russell.

ARNAUD MASSY: FIRST FOREIGNER TO WIN THE BRITISH OPEN

Arnaud Massy, a Frenchman, was the first foreigner to win the British Open when he captured the event at Hoylake in 1907. Massy started out as a left-handed golfer because he had been given a left-handed set as a beginner. In 1902, at the age of twenty-five, he began to play right handed. His first appearance in the British Open was in 1905, when he finished fifth. He won the French Open in 1906, 1907, 1911, and 1925. Massy also won one Belgian Open and three Spanish Opens.

Golf allegedly took a foothold on the European continent when Scottish regiments billeted at Pau, France, during the Peninsula War in 1814 played improvised games of golf on the Plain of Billere. After the war some of the Scots returned for a bit of holiday duffing near Pau, but it was not until 1856 that the Pau Golf Club was established, the first golf club on the Continent.

HAROLD HILTON: THE ONLY AMATEUR TO WIN TWO BRITISH OPENS

Harold Hilton (1869–1942) from West Kirby, Cheshire, England, is the only British amateur to win the British Open twice (1892, 1897). He also won four British Amateurs (1900, 1901, 1911, 1913) and the U.S. Amateur (1911). Hilton's 1892 British Open victory marked the first time the event had been held at Muirfield, and the first time it was played over seventy-two holes instead of thirty-six. Hilton's second Open win came at Hoylake. A powerfully built man approximately five feet, seven inches tall, Hilton had a fast swing but unusual control for someone who hit off his toes. He also had a deft putting stroke, was an excellent shot improviser, and had mastered the art of backspin. Hilton authored several books including *My Golfing Reminiscences,* and also served as editor of *Golf Illustrated.*

THE RISE OF
AMERICAN GOLF

THE "FIRST" AMERICAN GOLF CLUB

John Reid, born in Scotland in 1840, is often credited as the "Father of American Golf" even though golf was played in the colonial United States as early as the eighteenth century. Reid did not play the game until 1888 when, living in Westchester County, just north of New York City, he decided to try out a gift from fellow Scotsman Robert Lockhart, who had just returned to the United States from Saint Andrews. There, Lockhart had purchased twenty-four gutta-percha balls and six clubs—three woods and three irons—from Old Tom Morris. At the time Reid was manager of the J. L. Mott Iron Works at Mott Haven in the Bronx. He gathered five friends—John B. Upham, Henry Holbrook, Kingman H. Putnam, Henry O. Tallmadge, and Alexander P. W. Kinnan—and laid out three holes in a pasture in Yonkers. They eventually ordered more clubs and moved to a larger pasture, where they laid out six rough holes with bumpy greens approximately twelve feet in diameter. Later that year, on November 14, Reid invited his friends to a special dinner where they organized the Saint Andrews Golf Club, one of the five founding members of the United States Golf Association.

Various records, including newspaper accounts, indicate that forms of organized golf existed in America from the 1700s. A number of Scots migrated to Charleston and Savannah in 1736, for example. Many notices of the South Carolina Golf Club appeared in the press including the following notice in the October 13, 1795, *Charleston City Gazette:* "The anniversary of the Golf Club will be held on Saturday next at the Club House on Charleston's Green where the members are requested to attend at one o'clock." The South Carolina Golf Club was founded in Charleston in 1786.

THE FOUNDING OF THE UNITED STATES GOLF ASSOCIATION

In 1894 Theodore A. Havemeyer, an American "Sugar King" millionaire, was elected the first president of what was to become the United States Golf Association. He had been introduced to golf on a trip to France and later founded the Newport (Rhode Island) Golf Club with Cornelius Vanderbilt, John Jacob Astor, Oliver Belmont, and other wealthy Americans. The original name of the group was the Amateur Golf Association; then it added competitions that included professionals, and became the USGA. The founding clubs were Newport, Chicago, Saint Andrews, Shinnecock Hills (Southampton, New York), and The Country Club (Brookline, Massachusetts). The USGA is responsible, along with the R&A, for making decisions on the rules of golf and organizing competitions. Its national amateur championships for men and women include the Junior Amateur, U.S. Women's Amateur, U.S. Senior Amateur, and others. It also organizes international events such as the Curtis Cup and Walker Cup matches along with the U.S. Open. Shown here is Golf House, the USGA headquarters in Far Hills, New Jersey.

CHARLES BLAIR MACDONALD: AMERICAN GOLF PIONEER

C. B. Macdonald (1855–1939) was one of the early pioneers of organized American golf. He founded the Chicago Golf Club, a charter member of the USGA, and designed that club's course (1895), the National Golf Links (1911), and other excellent golf courses. Macdonald wrote the classic *Scotland's Gift: Golf* (1928) and is credited with winning the first U.S. Amateur at Newport in 1895—having lost the "unofficial" first U.S. Amateur in 1894. Macdonald was not a gracious loser. He arranged to have the 1894 event declared null and void because he deemed it not officially sanctioned by a golf governing body. The USGA, founded in December 1894, sanctioned the 1895 event.

Macdonald was the son of a Scottish father and Canadian mother. He grew up in Chicago but returned to his father's homeland in 1872 to attend the University of Saint Andrews. There he learned the game of golf under the tutelage of his grandfather and watched matches involving Old Tom Morris and other golf greats. It was his thirst for golf that moved him to design the Chicago Golf Club after his return from abroad. Macdonald had strong opinions on almost everything, especially the criteria for a great golf course. One of them is: "What a golfer most desires is variety in the one-, two- and three-shot holes, calling for accuracy in placing the ball, not alone in the approach but also from the tee. Let the first shot be played in relation to the second shot in accordance with the run of the ground and the wind. Holes so designed permit the player to, if he so wishes, take risks commensurate to the gravity of the situation."

WILLIE DUNN JR.: REMODELER OF SHINNECOCK

Willie Dunn Jr. was born in Musselburgh, Midlothian, Scotland, in 1870. He was a professional greenkeeper and course builder under his brother Tom, sixteen years his senior. He briefly served as a professional at Westward Ho! in 1886, then laid out the Chingford course near London before moving to Biarritz in France, where he helped his brother build a course and served as a pro. There he also met W. K. Vanderbilt, the American tycoon and golf enthusiast, and was persuaded to emigrate to the United States in 1891. With the help of the Shinnecock tribe and a commission from Vanderbilt, Dunn built the original twelve-hole Shinnecock Hills golf course on Long Island, New York. The course was enlarged to eighteen holes the following year. Dunn won the "unofficial" first U.S. Open—a match-play event with only four competitors. He was the runner-up in the first U.S. Open, held at the Newport (Rhode Island) Golf Club. That event, a thirty-six-hole stroke-play competition with a field of eleven golfers, was won by Horace Rawlins with a score of 173.

MRS. BROWN: FIRST WINNER OF THE U.S. WOMEN'S AMATEUR

Mrs. C. S. Brown carded a 132 in an eighteen-hole stroke-play event at the Meadow Brook Club in Hempstead, Long Island, New York, to win the first U.S. Women's Amateur Championship in 1895. There were thirteen contestants. Her scores on the last six holes of her first nine were 4, 5, 7, 9, 4, and 6; the quality of golf and the breadth of participation would soon improve, however. The following year an eighteen-hole stroke-play qualifier was held before a match-play tournament. This format continued until 1952. Currently the tournament format is a thirty-six hole stroke-play qualifier and a match-play tournament. The 1995 Championship had over 450 entrants.

**BEATRIX HOYT: WINNER OF THREE CON-
SECUTIVE U.S. AMATEURS**

Beatrix Hoyt was the outstanding female golfer
of the 1890s. At the age of sixteen she began her
streak of three consecutive U.S. Women's Amateur titles (1896, 1897, 1898). She won the medal
five years in succession with scores of 95 in 1896;
108 in 1897; 92 in 1898; 97 in 1899; and 94 in 1900. The fields
in these events were small—no more than sixteen in the match-
play finals after the eighteen-hole stroke-play qualifying round.
Most of the contestants were from the New York metropolitan
area. Miss Hoyt retired from tournament play at the age of
twenty.

PEBBLE BEACH, NO. 18

The 548-yard par-5 18th hole at Pebble Beach on California's Monterey Peninsula is one of the most scenic and famous finishing holes in golf.

© Mike Klemme/golfoto.com

PEBBLE BEACH, No.7

Pebble Beach, a 6,815-yard gem, was designed by golf amateur Jack Neville with Douglas Grant and opened in 1919. The 107-yard par-3 seventh hole can be played with any club from a wood to a wedge depending on the wind coming off the ocean.

© Mike Klemme/golfoto.com

St. Andrews, No. 18

Founded on May 14, 1754, the Royal and Ancient Club in the old Scottish University town of St. Andrews is set on a narrow strip of linksland and features seven huge double greens. *©1994 Russell Kirk*

Swilken Bridge, St. Andrews

The Swilken Bridge, one of three crossing a small stream cutting the linksland course at St. Andrews, can be traversed to reach the famous large double green at the 354-yard par-4 finishing hole called "Tom Morris." Jack Nicklaus hit his drive through this green in the 1970 British Open playoff against Doug Sanders, then got up and down for a birdie to win the second of his three British Open titles.

©1994 Russell Kirk

ROYAL TROON, NO. 8 "POSTAGE STAMP"

Royal Troon, on Scotland's Ayrshire coast, is a regular part of the
British Open rotation. The 126-yard "Postage Stamp" eighth
hole is a tiny target in a sea of sand. In 1950 German amateur
Herman Tissies took a fifteen and in 1973 the 71-year-old Gene
Sarazan scored an ace here in the British Open.

© 1994 Russell Kirk

Nick Faldo, one of England's greatest golfers, has been on eleven Ryder Cup teams and has won six major titles, the British Open (1987, 1990, 1992) and the Masters (1989, 1990, 1996). © *Montana Pritchard/PGA of America*

Jack Nicklaus, considered by many the best golfer of all time, has won twenty major tournaments, including two U.S. Amateurs, six Masters, five PGA's, four U.S. Opens, and three British Opens. © *USGA/Robert Walker*

Tiger Woods, shown here with his coach Butch Harmon, won three consecutive U.S. Amateurs before turning professional in 1996. In his first full professional season he won the 1997 Masters at age 21 and led the PGA Tour in earnings. *Gerald Sprayregen*

Arnold Palmer, one of the most charismatic golfers ever to play the game, has 60 tour victories, including four Masters, two British Opens, and one U.S. Open. He has a record twenty-two Ryder Cup match victories. © *Daniel Dmitruck/USGA*

Nancy Lopez is a 47-time winner on the LPGA Tour and is a member of its exclusive Hall of Fame. She won nine tournaments in 1978, including a record five in a row. © *USGA/J.D. Cuban*

Tiger Woods tees off at the 1997 British Open at Royal Troon. *Gerald Sprayregen.*

AUGUSTA NATIONAL, NO. 13

Augusta National, a 6,925-yard par-72 designed by Robert Tyre Jones, Jr. and Alister Mackenzie, opened in 1933 and became the annual site of The Masters, golf's rite of spring. The 485-yard par-5 "Azalea" hole (No. 13) is the final hole of "Amen Corner."
© Mike Klemme/golfoto.com

SHINNECOCK HILLS, NO. 16

Shinnecock Hills, a 6,697-yard par-70 etched in the sand dunes of eastern Long Island, New York was originally designed by Willie Dunn and opened in 1891. The 513-yard par-5 sixteenth is backed by its venerable clubhouse, built in 1892 and designed by Stanford White.

© Mike Klemme/golfoto.com

BALTUSROL

In 1918, Baltusrol hired A.W. Tillinghast to build two golf courses, the Upper and Lower, that were to make Baltusrol one of the best championship golf sites in the world. Set in Springfield, New Jersey, Baltusrol has hosted the U.S. Women's Amateur, the U.S. Women's Open, and the U.S. Open. © *Mike Klemme/golfoto.com*

PGA WEST STADIUM COURSE, No. 17

The PGA West Stadium course, a Pete Dye design in La Quinta, California. The 166-yard par-3 seventeenth is called "Alcatraz" because there is no bailout. © *Mike Klemme/golfoto.com*

AMERICAN GOLF: A THREAT TO THE OLD WORLD?

In 1902 the London and County Professional Golfers' Association was formed—largely in reaction to the strong growth of American golf. The British were concerned that the advent of the Haskell ball, patented in 1899 in the United States, would lead to the decline of the ball-remolding and -repainting business of the golf professional. The Britons were also concerned that their players were being lured to the lucrative golf market in the United States. The sport was spreading throughout the world, much of it on the wave of the British Empire. Calcutta, the forerunner of Royal Calcutta, was formed in 1829; the Royal Bombay (India) Golfing Society (1842), Royal Adelaide Golf Club in Australia (1870), Royal Montreal Golf Club in Canada (1873), and the Royal Cape Golf Club at Wynberg, South Africa (1885), are a few more examples of this trend.

By 1900 the United States had over one thousand golf courses, more than the rest of the world combined. Shinnecock Hills in Southampton, Long Island, pictured here, featured the first U.S. clubhouse. This masterpiece was designed by Stanford White and constructed in 1891. The club, named after the local Shinnecock tribe, was reportedly the first to have been incorporated and the first to have a waiting list. Public golf also began to flourish. The Van Cortlandt golf course in New York City became the United States' first municipal golf course when it opened in 1895. Among the more than fifteen thousand golf courses in the country today, approximately twenty-three hundred are municipal golf courses. The rest are categorized as private or daily-fee courses. There are currently over twenty-five million golfers in the United States.

GOLF JOURNALISM

Golf, published in Great Britain in 1890, was the first magazine for golfers. *The Golfer,* the first American golf magazine, debuted in New York in 1894. During the 1929 U.S. Amateur at Pebble Beach, the *New York Times* writer William D. Richardson proposed the idea of a golf writers' association. The idea lay fallow until 1946, when the Golf Writers Association of America was founded. Herb Graffis, pictured center, with golfers Horton Smith (left) and Walter Hagen, was president of the association (1951–52); other notable writers served later, including Grantland Rice, Dick Taylor, and Furman Bishop. Graffis established *Golfdom,* a trade magazine, in 1927, and was editor of *Golfing,* a magazine that was sold to *Golf* in the 1960s. In 1936 Herb, his brother Joe, and others established the National Golf Foundation to promote the growth and vitality of golf. Golf is now widely reported on through many media including newspapers, magazines, newsletters, books, television, video, software, and the Internet.

GOLF RESORTS: PIONEERING AT PINEHURST

One of the earliest and finest destination resorts began in 1895 when Boston philanthropist James Walker Tufts purchased fifty-five hundred acres of timberland on sandy soil in North Carolina. He was interested in building a luxury health resort and called the spot Tuftstown. It was eventually renamed Pinehurst, after the area's magnificent trees and *hurst,* "a wooded plot on rising ground." The firm headed by Frederick Law Olmsted, architect and designer of Central Park in New York City, was hired to design and landscape Pinehurst. The Pinehurst Hotel, pictured here (originally the Carolina Hotel), opened in 1901, and recreational activities, including eight golf courses, were added over the years. Today Pinehurst has eight golf courses and is still among the top-rated golf resorts in the world.

DONALD ROSS: AMERICA'S FIRST DOMI-NANT GOLF COURSE ARCHITECT

Donald Ross was born in Dornoch, Scotland, in 1872; he learned club making in an apprenticeship at David Forgan's shop in Saint Andrews and studied golf under Old Tom Morris. He later returned to Dornoch to serve as professional and greenkeeper, where he learned grass maintenance and hole design. In 1899 he emigrated to the Boston area, where he served as a professional and greenkeeper at the Oakley Club, whose membership included the wealthy Tufts family. James W. Tufts persuaded Ross to design his Pinehurst Resort golf courses in North Carolina. The acclaim gained by Pinehurst, and Ross's highly regarded No. 2 Course at the resort, put Ross at the forefront of American golf course architecture. He based his practice in Pinehurst from 1912 until his death in 1948. Ross's courses include Seminole (1929) in Florida; Oakland Hills (North, 1923; South 1927) in Michigan; Pine Needles (1927) in North Carolina; and many others. The subtlety of Ross's crowned greens, the contour and placement of his bunkers, and the strategic design of his courses are studied by most serious modern golf course architects.

WALTER TRAVIS: SELF-MADE CHAMPION

Walter Travis (1862–1927) was born in Australia, but emigrated to the United States and took up the game of golf at age thirty-five. He was a self-made golfer who was not long off the tee. He often found himself hitting woods and long irons to reach par 4s and 5s in regulation. But he had a center-shafted Schenectady putter and he was deadly around the greens. Some golf purists thought the Schenectady a form of golf blasphemy. The British banned the club after Travis used it to win the 1904 British Amateur at Royal Saint George's in Sandwich, Kent. The Schenectady club, which Travis had borrowed from a friend one day before the Championship, was not reinstated there until almost fifty years later. In reality Travis won the Amateur with his controlled compact swing, judgment of distance, club selection, and consistency which all served him well on the windy links of Kent.

Travis also won three U.S. Amateurs (1900, 1901, 1903). His other golf interests included golf course design and journalism. Travis founded and edited *The American Golfer* and designed the Garden City (Long Island, New York) Golf Club—site of the 1924 Walker Cup, the 1936 U.S. Amateur, and other important golf events. His last tournament win was the 1915 New York Metropolitan Amateur, at which he calmly dropped a thirty-foot putt to clinch his victory.

**JERRY TRAVERS: WINNER OF FOUR U.S. AMA-
TEURS**

Jerry Travers was a dominant amateur golfer at a time
when many of the best American amateurs came out of
the Northeast. The son of a wealthy New York family, Travers won five Metropolitan Amateurs (1906, 1907, 1911,
1912, 1913), four U.S. Amateurs (1907, 1908, 1912,
1913), and the 1915 U.S. Open. Though short off the tee,
Travers was unperturbed under duress and was an excellent recovery player with a deadly short game. Travers
played when the spirit moved him. After winning the U.S.
Open at Baltusrol, he didn't bother to defend his title the
following year.

FRANCIS OUIMET: PUTS AMERICAN GOLF ON THE WORLD MAP

Francis Ouimet (right) and Charles (Chick) Evans (left) lent tremendous stature to American golf at a time when U.S. national championships were dominated by British-born golfers. Ouimet, then a twenty-year-old former caddie, stunned the golf world in 1913 when he defeated the great British professionals Harry Vardon and Ted Ray in a playoff for the U.S. Open Championship at The Country Club in Brookline, Massachusetts.

With Walter Travis's win in the 1904 British Amateur and Johnny McDermott's successive wins in the 1911 and 1912 U.S. Opens, the Americans were serving notice that they could compete in the international arena dominated by the British since the beginning of organized golf.

Charles Evans won both the U.S. Open and the U.S. Amateur in 1916. Previously he had won the Western Open (1910), then considered second in stature to the U.S. Open. Evans played in seven U.S. Amateurs before he won his first, largely because of putting problems. He won another Amateur in 1920 and would win six Western Amateurs plus the French Amateur (1911) and the North and South Amateur (1911) in his outstanding career. He played in fifty consecutive national championships and almost won a third U.S. Amateur in 1927—but Bobby Jones, who scored seven 3s in eleven holes, thwarted him. Before he retired, Evans, who had been a caddie, set up a scholarship fund at Northwestern University to financially assist college-bound caddies.

THE FOUNDING OF THE PROFESSIONAL GOLFERS ASSOCIATION OF AMERICA

The Professional Golfers Association of America (PGA) was formed in 1916 in New York by businessmen and amateur golfers, most notably Rodman Wannamaker, for whom the PGA championship trophy is named. The Tour, then a loose and informal array of tournaments, began in the early 1920s with a lineup that featured Walter Hagen, Jim Barnes, Jock Hutchinson, Tommy McNamara, Bobby Cruickshank, and other drawing cards.

In the old days, professionals were disdained by many of the amateurs as lacking in formal education and being socially unsophisticated. Now most professionals come out of college programs, the minor leagues of the PGA, and to become club professionals must be skilled in instruction, management, merchandising, communications, and other facets of modern golf management. The PGA offers a variety of training and continuing education programs to promote professionalism.

The seeds of the Tour were likely planted in Florida, where informal tournaments were held prior to World War I. Tournaments generally started when a promoter put up some prize money and some leading professionals—perhaps Walter Hagen, Tommy Armour, or Long Jim Barnes—agreed to participate. The summer Tour circuit started in 1930, but it was not until 1936 that the PGA hired a full-time tournament director, Fred Corcoran. By 1946, when he left to become involved in the nascent LPGA Tour, the prize money had grown to $750,000. Tournament dates grew from eleven to thirty.

Pictured here is Jim Barnes, winner of the first PGA Championship played at the Siwanoy Country Club in Bronxville, New York. Barnes also won the second PGA Championship, held in 1919 after World War I.

THE COLOR BAN IN PROFESSIONAL GOLF

Article Three, Section One of the PGA Constitution of 1916 stated that eligibility for the organization required being a member of the Caucasian race. In 1928 the United Golf Association, the black equivalent of the PGA, was formed and headquartered in Stowe, Massachusetts. It was not until 1961 that the Caucasians-only clause was deleted from the PGA Constitution and African American and other minority professionals were accepted onto the Tour. Charlie Sifford, pictured here, was one of the best black players there and the first black player to win an official Tour event—the 1967 Hartford Open.

JOHN SHIPPEN

The first non-Caucasian entrant in a major U.S. golf tournament was John Shippen, shown here, part West Indian and part Shinnecock, who competed in the 1896 U.S. Open. He was tied for first after the first round and finished fifth in that thirty-six-hole stroke-play event.

LADY GOLF
PIONEERS

GOLF FUND RAISING

During World War I golf began its long association with charitable organizations. The Red Cross conducted exhibitions and charged admission fees to competitions, which often featured fine women golfers of the period, among them Glenna Collett, Edith Cummings, Marion Hollins, Maureen Orcutt, Miriam Burns, Virginia Van Wie, Mary K. Brown, and Helen Hicks.

Admission fees were first charged at the 1922 U.S. Open at the Skokie Country Club near Chicago. Soon all professional events charged admission fees, with much of the money earmarked for charity. By 1997 the PGA had generated over three hundred million dollars for charities from Tour events.

Alexa Stirling, pictured here, won the U.S. Women's Amateur in 1916, 1919, and 1920. In 1917, with Elaine Rosenthal, Perry Adair, and Bobby Jones (a fellow Georgian), she toured the eastern United States giving charity exhibition matches that raised $150,000 for the Red Cross.

GREAT WOMEN GOLFERS: WETHERED AND VARE

Joyce Wethered, born in England in 1901 and pictured at left is one of the best lady golfers of all time. She won four consecutive English Ladies' (1920–1923) and four British Ladies' (1922, 1924, 1925, 1929). She was noted for her smooth swing and her great distance off the tee. Her ability to concentrate and successfully play one hole at a time in head-to-head match play is legendary.

Bobby Jones claimed she was the best golfer, man or woman, he had ever seen. Jones commented on her swing in the July 1930 issue of *The American Golfer:* "To describe her manner of playing is almost impossible. She stands quite close to the ball, she places the club once behind, takes one look toward the objective and strikes. Her swing is not long—surprisingly short, indeed, when one considers the power she develops—but it is rhythmic to the last degree. She makes ample use of her wrists, and her left arm within the hitting area is firm and active. This, I think, distinguishes her swing from that of any other woman golfer, and it is the one thing that makes her the player she is."

GLENNA COLLETT VARE

One of Wethered's most formidable opponents was Glenna Collett Vare, one of America's best golfers, pictured here at Pebble Beach in 1928. Born in New Haven, Connecticut, in 1903, Mrs. Vare won a record six U.S. Women's Amateurs (1922, 1925, 1928, 1929, 1930, 1935). In the 1929 British Ladies', Wethered defeated Vare (then Glenna Collett) 3 and 1. Vare was on the original Curtis Cup team in 1932, and every year the Vare Trophy is awarded to the LPGA player with the best scoring average. Patty Berg first won this honor in 1953 with a 75.0 average. Karrie Webb won it in 1997 with a 70.0 average.

CECIL LEITCH

Charlotte Cecilia Pitcairn Leitch, better known as Cecil, brought power and competitive flair to women's golf at the beginning of the twentieth century. Born in Siloth, Cumberland, England, in 1891, Miss Leitch won twelve national titles: two English Ladies', five French Opens, four British Ladies', and the Canadian Ladies' Open. Her battles with Joyce Wethered raised the level of interest in women's golf and elevated the level of play. Wethered's victory over Leitch, 2 and 1, in the finals of the English Ladies' Amateur at Sheringham in 1920 ended Leitch's dominance of British women's golf. Wethered was a nineteen-year-old unknown prior to her victory.

ENID WILSON: CHAMPION AND GOLF JOURNALIST

Enid Wilson is considered the second-best British woman golfer between the wars—after Joyce Wethered. Born in Stonebroom, Derbyshire, England, in 1910, Wilson won the British Girls' in 1925, four Lower Midland Women's (1926, 1928, 1929, 1930), three British Ladies' (1931, 1932, 1933), and was a member of Britain's first Curtis Cup team in 1932. She took up golf writing after World War II, contributing to the *Daily Telegraph* for many years. Her book *A Gallery of Women Golfers* (1961) is one of the best on women's golf.

THE CURTIS CUP

The Curtis Cup is named for Harriot and Margaret Curtis, American golfing sisters who both won the American Women's National Amateur Championship. The event had its origins in 1905 when Frances Griscom of Philadelphia suggested it would be fun for a group to play in the British Women's Championship at Cromer, England. Eight players from the United States went, including four championship-level players: Miss Griscom, Georgianna Bishop, and the Curtis sisters. Prior to the British Women's, an informal match was held between the British and the American sides—the first international match between the two. The British won easily but the Curtis sisters felt that an amateur international women's team competition should be held on a regular basis. It took until 1932 for the their dream to be realized.

The Curtis Cup competition is an amateur team event held every two years between the British and Irish team and the Americans. The first Curtis Cup match was played at the Wentworth Golf Club (East Course) in England in 1932 and was won by the United States team, 5½ to 3½. Three foursome matches and six singles contests were played. The United States won the first six contests before the British and Irish finally took the cup in 1952.

The Curtis Cup format is now six foursomes and twelve singles matches played over a two-day period. The matches are held every two years at alternating team "home" sites.

Pictured here (l. to r.) are Harriot and Margaret Curtis.

GOLF'S LIGHTER SIDE

Patty Berg, Betty Mims Danoff, Babe Zaharias and Louise Suggs hamming it up on the road in the early days of the LPGA Tour.

HOGAN, NELSON & SNEAD:
GOLF COMES OF AGE

INTERNATIONAL COMPETITION: THE WALKER CUP

The Walker Cup was donated in 1920 by George Herbert Walker, president of the USGA. Walker, a low-handicap player at the National Golf Links of America, was part of the USGA's delegation at a coordinating meeting with the Royal and Ancient on the rules of golf in the spring of 1920. It was Walker who, as president of the USGA, had to reprimand Bobby Jones, then nineteen, for throwing his club and grazing a fan after sculling his shot at a critical point in the 1921 U.S. Amateur at the Saint Louis Country Club. Walker wrote to Jones: "You will never play in a USGA event unless you can control your temper." Jones went on to control his temper; he is shown here putting in his 1930 Walker Cup match against Roger Wethered, captain of the British and Irish side, held at Royal St. George's Golf Club, Sandwich, England. Jones won this contest, 9 and 8, and the United States won the match, 10 and 2.

The first match-play competition between male amateurs from Great Britain and Ireland and those from the United States was held at the National Golf Links in Southampton, New York, and was won by 8 and 4 by the U.S.. Great Britain and Ireland first won this biannual event in 1938 at Saint Andrews, Scotland. Overall, Great Britain and Ireland has won four matches of the thirty-six held through 1997. The Walker Cup format now includes eight alternating-shot foursomes and sixteen singles matches played over a two-day period.

THE RYDER CUP

Samuel Ryder (left), a flower and seed merchant from Saint Albans, Hertfordshire, England, took up golf in his early 50's under the guidance of noted professional Abe Mitchell. After Britain won an unofficial match against a group of American professionals, 13$\frac{1}{2}$ to 1$\frac{1}{2}$ at Wentworth in 1926, Ryder presented a solid gold trophy for a formal international series. Walter Hagen led the American team to a decisive 9$\frac{1}{2}$ to 2$\frac{1}{2}$ win in the first official contest held at the Worcester Country Club in Massachusetts in 1927. The competition now includes European Tour members, and the match-play format includes four foursomes and four four-ball matches on the first and second days, then ten singles matches on the final day, for a total of 28 points.

Ryder is shown here presenting the 1929 Ryder Cup to victorious British captain George Duncan.

WALTER HAGEN: WINNER OF FOUR CONSECUTIVE PGA CHAMPIONSHIPS

One of the great raconteurs and competitors in golf was Walter Hagen (1892–1969), a native of Rochester, New York. An ambidextrous baseball pitcher with promise, Hagen reluctantly gave up his dream of becoming a major-league baseball player to concentrate on golf. He started out as a caddie at the Country Club of Rochester and entered his first major tournament, the U.S. Open, in 1913. There he finished a respectable fourth, but all the attention was directed toward amateur Francis Ouimet, who outdueled Vardon and Ray in that fabled playoff showdown at The Country Club in Brookline, Massachusetts. Hagen appeared in that tournament in the sartorial splendor that was to be his trademark—adorned with checked Scottish cap, a colorful bandanna, striped silk shirt, white flannels, and white shoes with tongues carefully folded at the instep. Later he moved up to monogrammed silk shirts, custom-made shoes and an entourage that included a chauffeur, manager, and caddie. Hagen played golf with attitude, the firm belief that he had the shots to win, especially in match play.

Hagen had the game to back himself up. He won four consecutive PGA titles (1924-1927) after winning his first PGA Championship, then a match-play event, in 1921. He won forty PGA events in all, along with over twenty other tournaments at a time when there were relatively few professional tournaments with national and international participation. This places him at the top of the list of American professional golfers who completed their careers before World War II. He won the U.S. Open in 1914 and 1919, four British Opens (1922, 1924, 1928, 1929) , five Western Opens (1916, 1921, 1926, 1927, 1932), and the 1931 Canadian Open. Hagen played in every Ryder Cup championship, including the unofficial 1921 event, until 1937. He was the only team captain on the U.S. side until Ben Hogan took over that role in 1947.

Hagen was noted for his aforementioned flamboyance along with his determination to gain respect, and additional prize money, for professional golfers at a time when they were considered outcasts by many gentlemen players. Most clubs did not even let professionals into the clubhouse, and Hagen made his annoyance over this practice well known. He declined to enter the clubhouse for the British Open victory presentation at Troon in 1923 because professionals had not been allowed on the premises during tournament week.

Along with Babe Ruth, Bobby Jones, Red Grange, and others from the "Golden Age of Sport" in the 1920s, Hagen lent flair and excitement to his game. He paved the way for the professional game, causing Gene Sarazen to say: "Golf never had a showman like him. All the professionals who have a chance to go after big money today should say a silent thanks to Walter every time they stretch a check between their fingers. Walter made pro golf what it is."

Hagen is pictured here with his Cadillac in front of the Wilshire Country Club in Los Angeles in the 1930s.

GENE SARAZEN:
AUTHOR OF <u>THE SHOT HEARD ROUND THE WORLD</u>

Gene Sarazen, a first-generation American, shown here inaugurating night golf in Briarcliff Manor, New York, in 1924, was born Eugene Saraceni in 1902 in Harrison, New York. One of his most memorable achievements was his famed double-eagle 2 on the par-5 fifteenth hole at Augusta National in 1935, a shot that put The Masters on the international golf map. Among the few people to witness that 4-wood shot were Walter Hagen and Bobby Jones. Sarazen won that tournament plus two U.S. Opens (1922, 1932), three PGA Championships (1922, 1933, 1933), and the 1932 British Open. Sarazen, Walter Hagen, and Bobby Jones were leaders in the growth and international competitiveness of American golf after World War I. Bobby Jones characterized Sarazen as "the impatient player who went for everything in the hope of feeling the timely touch of inspiration. . . . The boldness of his play leaves no middle ground. When he is in the right mood, he is probably the greatest scorer in the game, possibly that the game has ever seen."

Sarazen, short and stocky, had a short, compact swing befitting his physique. He liked thick handles on his clubs but had small, beefy hands, so he held the club with his left hand in a "baseball" grip, interlocking the little finger of his right hand with the index finger of his left. A poor bunker player at the beginning, he designed the first modern sand wedge.

BOBBY JONES: GOLF'S GOLDEN AMATEUR

Bobby Jones (1902–1971) is the classic example of someone who brought intellect, grace, athletic prowess, competitive fire, and high ethical standards to the game. Jones, a native of Atlanta, is the only person to win four major championships ("The Grand Slam") in one year: The British Open, British Amateur, U.S. Amateur, and U.S. Open. (The Grand Slam now consists of The Masters, U.S. Open, British Open and PGA Championship.) After achieving this in 1930, at the age of twenty-eight, Jones, a part-time amateur golfer who seldom practiced, retired from major tournament competition to practice law.

A golf prodigy as a youth, Jones won thirteen major titles over a span of eight years: four U.S. Opens, five U.S. Amateurs, three British Opens, and the British Amateur. A Renaissance golf man, Jones co-authored (with O. B. Keeler) *Down the Fairway* (1927), one of the best golf books ever written, and was codesigner, with Alister Mackenzie, of Augusta National, one of the best golf courses in the world. After retiring from tournament golf, he developed a series of excellent golf instructional films that remain classics, and he was a founder of The Masters golf tournament, now a major international event.

Jones held degrees in English Literature (Harvard) and Mechanical Engineering (Georgia Tech); he also studied law at Emory University in Atlanta. Felled by a debilitating muscular disease in the 1950s, Jones was confined to a wheelchair thereafter. He refused to accept pity or express self-pity, proclaiming that he had to accept his fate, much the way a golfer must play his ball from where it lays.

Bobby Jones is the only athlete to have been honored with two ticker-tape parades down Broadway in New York City. He is pictured here with his four Grand Slam trophies from 1930.

THE TEACHING PROFESSIONAL

Stewart Maiden was born in Carnoustie, Scotland, in 1886 and emigrated to the United States in 1908; he became a professional at East Lake in Atlanta and instructed local prodigies Bobby Jones, Alexa Stirling, and others. Maiden served as a diagnostician of Jones's swing, which was patterned after his own: a rounded, smooth, and upright swing of the "Forfarshire School" in Carnoustie. He is shown here, at left, with Bobby Jones.

Maiden was an example of the great teaching professionals from the British Isles who brought the finer points of the game to Americans desiring to learn this newly popular sport. Eventually a cadre of American professionals would evolve to develop their own golf schools or become swing doctors to the rich and famous. Modern practitioners of the trade have included Butch Harmon, Jim Flick, David Leadbetter, Jim McLean, Peggy Kirk Bell, John Jacobs, Harvey Penick, Ken Venturi, and many others, all listed among *Golf* and *Golf Digest* magazines' annual roll of best teachers.

THE GOLF GLOVE AND HENRY COTTON

The left-handed golf glove was a rarity before the 1930s. Henry Cotton was one of the earliest professionals to regularly use one. Cotton defended Britain's golf honor at a time when the British were not winning many international majors, winning the British Open in 1934, 1937, and 1948. He was a three-time Ryder Cup contestant (1929, 1937, 1947) and a winner of the Belgian Open (1930, 1934, 1938), Italian Open (1936), Czechoslovak Open (1937, 1938), German Open (1937, 1938, 1939) and French Open (1946, 1947).

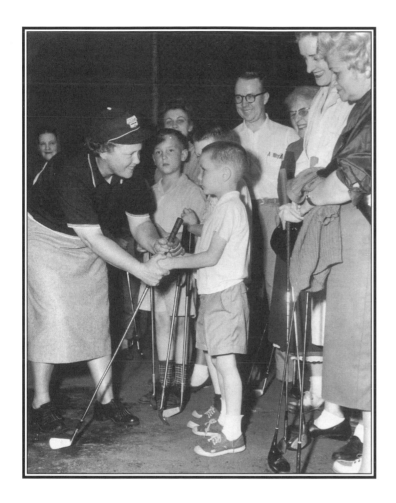

PATTY BERG: WINNER OF THE FIRST U.S. OPEN

Patty Berg, born in Minnesota in 1918, was a child athletic prodigy who took up the game of golf at age thirteen. She won the Minneapolis city Championship three years later, then went on to win twenty-eight amateur titles in seven years, including the 1938 U.S. Amateur. Miss Berg turned professional in 1940, was a charter member of the LPGA, and served as its first president (1949–1952). She won the first U.S. Women's Open in 1946 and still holds the record for winning the most women's majors—seven Titleholders, seven Western Opens, and her U.S. Open win. (Now the ladies' majors are the McDonald's LPGA Championship, U.S. Open, Du Maurier Classic, and Nabisco Dinah Shore.) Miss Berg has won a total of fifty-one professional tournaments and was among the four original inductees into the LPGA Hall of Fame in 1951, along with Betty Jameson, Louise Suggs, and Babe Didrikson Zaharias.

Entry into the LPGA Hall of Fame is considered to be one of the most difficult achievements in today's world of sports. Prerequisites for membership are that a player must have been a member in good standing of the association for ten consecutive years and have won at least thirty official events, including two major championships; thirty-five official events with one major championship title; or forty official Tour events exclusive of any major championship. Only fourteen players have made the Hall of Fame. In addition to the four founding members, they are Pat Bradley, JoAnne Carner, Sandra Haynie, Betsy King, Nancy Lopez, Carol Mann, Betsy Rawls, Patty Sheehan, Kathy Whitworth, and Mickey Wright.

WATER GOLF

While many golfers take the game seriously, there are others who just want to have fun. Above is a water golf course at the Huntington Hotel Pool in Pasadena, California, circa 1934.

GOLF ON TELEVISION

The BBC Television organization covered its first golf match at Roehampton in Southwest London in 1938. The essence of these early telecasts is captured in the photograph above.

Shell's Wonderful World of Golf, first aired in the United States in the 1960s, chronicled matches between international champions at sites around the world. After a hiatus, the series has been televised again in the 1990s. Among the contestants have been Gene Sarazen, Byron Nelson, Arnold Palmer, Jack Nicklaus, Greg Norman, Nick Faldo, and many others. Now dedicated television channels, most notably The Golf Channel—a business venture including Arnold Palmer—have added to golf coverage and interest in the game.

FRED CORCORAN: PGA AND LPGA PIONEER PROMOTER

Fred Corcoran, a native of Cambridge, Massachusetts, was one of golf's first advisers and agents. He became an agent and business manager for Ted Williams, Stan Musial, Babe Didrikson Zaharias, and other athletes. Corcoran also became executive director of the PGA, at a time when the professionals felt the organization was biased toward club professionals and not capable of developing, expanding, and managing a tour.

Corcoran served the PGA from 1936 to 1946, when he left to pursue his own business interests as an agent and business manager. He helped organize the LPGA and served as its director from 1949 to 1961. Babe Zaharias, Corcoran's business client, was the top draw on that nascent tour until she succumbed to cancer in 1956. Corcoran was also a founder of the Golf Writers' Association of America.

In the accompanying picture, from left to right, Fred Corcoran joins Johnny Revolta and Sam Byrd for a bit of practice under rainy conditions at the 1941 Crosby Pro-Amateur, then held at Rancho Santa Fe, California.

MARION HOLLINS: THE BUILDER OF PASATIEMPO

Marion Hollins (1893–1944) was the only daughter in a family with four boys in East Islip, Long Island, New York. An outstanding athlete at a young age, Hollins was the first woman to enter and drive an automobile in the Vanderbilt Cup races, then a major event on Long Island. She was instrumental in finding financing for the Woman's National Golf and Country Club in Glen Head, Long Island. An excellent golfer, Hollins won the 1921 U.S. Amateur and was the captain of the first Curtis Cup team in 1932.

Hollins moved west to become athletic director at Cypress Point and persuaded Dr. Alister Mackenzie to design the course, which opened in 1928. Her long-term goal was to build a golf course and sports center, which she did at Pasatiempo in Santa Cruz with $2.5 million she made on a $100,000 investment in Kettleman Oil near Bakersfield. Hollins retained Alister Mackenzie to design her golf course within a 570-acre parcel of land in Santa Cruz.

Hollins was a pioneer in golf course real-estate development but lost her fortune in the Depression. The course and surrounding real-estate development have recovered under new ownership, however, and Pasatiempo is now rated one of the best golf courses in the United States.

BABE DIDRIKSON ZAHARIAS: OLYMPIAN AND GOLF CHAMPION

Mildred "Babe" Didrikson Zaharias, born in Port Arthur, Texas, was the greatest female athlete ever to compete on the LPGA Tour. She won two track and field medals in the 1932 Olympics in Los Angeles and excelled at other sports, including basketball and baseball. Babe first played a round of golf at the advanced age of twenty-eight. She recalled that day in her book, *The Life I've Led*, published in 1955: "A majority of my drives that day were between 240 and 260 yards. Of course, I had some bad shots in between. I've read since then that my score for the round was eighty-six. Actually I think it was around 100." She won the U.S. Women's Amateur in 1946 and the British Ladies' in 1947—the first American to win the British Ladies'.

The Babe had flair and drew huge crowds. Her box office appeal helped establish the nascent LPGA Tour in the 1950s. She won the first two official LPGA money titles: $14,800 in 1950 and $15,087 in 1951. The Babe also won three U.S. Women's Opens, three Titleholders, and four Western Opens to give her ten majors, fourth best on the all-time LPGA list. She won 31 of the 128 LPGA events she entered during her short eight-year career.

A measure of Babe's character is her courageous battle against cancer. She had surgery in 1953 then won her third Open by twelve strokes in 1954. She died in 1956 at the age of forty-two.

LOUISE SUGGS: CHARTER MEMBER OF THE LPGA HALL OF FAME

Louise Suggs, a native of Atlanta, Georgia, had an excellent amateur career, winning the Georgia State Amateur in 1940 and 1942; the Southern Amateur Championship in 1941 and 1947; the 1947 U.S. Amateur; the 1948 British Amateur; and the North/South Championship in 1942, 1946, and 1948. She was a member of the U.S. Curtis Cup team before she turned professional in 1948.

A founding member of the LPGA, she won fifty tournaments on the Tour, including the U.S. Women's Open (1949, 1952); the Western Open (1946, 1947, 1949, 1953); the Titleholders (1946, 1954, 1956, 1959); and the LPGA Championship (1957). She ranks third—behind Patty Berg and Mickey Wright—with eleven major titles. Her best money-earning year was 1953 when she earned $19,568 and won five tournaments.

Suggs was inducted into the LPGA Hall of Fame in 1951.

BETTY JAMESON: WINNER OF THE SECOND U.S. OPEN AND CHARTER HALL OF FAMER

Betty Jameson, born in Norman, Oklahoma, was an LPGA pioneer who won the second U.S. Women's Open in 1947. Prior to turning professional she won two U.S. Amateurs (1939, 1940). She was a superb golf technician who disciplined her swing so that she could build a solid stance, take a slightly upright backswing, and smoothly accelerate through the ball. She was noted for her ability to keep the ball in play, enabling her to win fourteen amateur tournament before turning professional. She originated the idea of annually honoring the golfer with the best scoring average on the LPGA Tour and, in 1952, donated a trophy to that cause in the name of Glenna Collett Vare. She was among the four best professional golfers of her era, along with Patty Berg, Louise Suggs, and Babe Zaharias.

BEN HOGAN: THE WEE ICE MAN

Ben Hogan was born in Texas in 1912 and died in Texas in 1997; he was affectionately known as *Bantam Ben* because he weighed in at 140 pounds during his prime. Hogan was a steel-willed competitor who ground it out on the practice range, where he overcame a severe hook and went on to win The Masters (1951, 1953); British Open (1953); U.S. Open (1948, 1950, 1951, 1953); and PGA (1946, 1948). He is one of four players (along with Gene Sarazen, Gary Player and Jack Nicklaus) to have won four of the world's modern major titles.

In 1949 Hogan was almost killed in an automobile accident, but recovered to play in the 1950 Los Angeles Open; later that year he won the U.S. Open at Merion in a playoff with Lloyd Mangrum and George Fazio. One of his noteworthy losses was in the 1955 U.S. Open at the Olympic Club in San Francisco, when he lost in a playoff to Jack Fleck, then an obscure club professional. Hogan was noted for his stoic professionalism; he was also nicknamed the Wee Ice Man by the Scots, because of his coolness under tournament pressure. His book, *Five Lessons: The Modern Fundamentals of Golf,* with Herbert Warren Wind, is considered an instructional classic. Hogan's sixty-three PGA Tour wins places him third on the all-time list, behind Snead and Nicklaus.

SAM SNEAD: THE ALL-TIME PGA VICTORY CHAMPION

Sam Snead is sometimes known as the greatest player never to have won the U.S. Open. By comparison, he thus sometimes unfairly takes a backseat to his contemporaries Ben Hogan and Byron Nelson. But Snead has won more PGA Tour victories (eighty-one) than anyone else, including three Masters (1949, 1952, 1954) and three PGA Championships (1942, 1949, 1951). He won the British Open in 1946 and finished second in the U.S. Open four times. Raised in the hills around Hot Springs, Virginia, Snead was noted for his classic, smooth swing which enabled him to play competitive PGA Tour golf into his early fifties. He won his last regular Tour event in 1965—the Greensboro Open—at the age of fifty-three.

BYRON NELSON: HOLDER OF GOLF'S CONSECUTIVE TOUR-NAMENT WINS RECORD

Byron Nelson is among the retinue of great golfers to come out of the state of Texas, joining Ben Hogan, Lee Trevino, Jimmy Demaret, Jack Burke Jr., Babe Zaharias, Kathy Whitworth, Ben Crenshaw, Tom Kite, and others. Born in 1912, the same year as Hogan and Snead, Nelson still holds the amazing record of eleven consecutive Tour event wins, set in 1945. Of the thirty-one tournaments he played in that year, Nelson won eighteen and was second seven times. For his season efforts he led the Tour in earnings with $63,335.66, paid to him in War Bonds. There were thirty-six events with total purses of $435,380 in 1945; by 1997 there were forty-five events, valued at over $75 million.

Nelson won five majors: The Masters (1937, 1942); the U.S. Open (1939); and the PGA Championship (1940, 1945). He achieved a 68.33 stroke average in 1945; today the PGA Tour stroke average award is known as the Byron Nelson Award. Over six feet in height with huge hands, Nelson was a superb long-iron player with a swing so fluid it was used as the model for Iron Byron, the USGA's mechanical golf ball striking machine, which sets standards for golf balls.

THE AMERICAN SOCI-
ETY OF GOLF COURSE
ARCHITECTS

In 1947 the American
Society of Golf Course
Architects was founded,
and joined by 1990 with
the European Association
of Golf Architects. As golf technology and business practices became more sophisticated, the
American Society of Golf Course Architects developed strategies and committees (on such topics
as environmental concerns and professional development) to address the challenges of the chang-
ing game.

Among the golf course architects gathered here are George C. Thomas Jr. (third from the left);
Alister Mackenzie (center), and, second from the right, William P. Bell. Thomas and Bell designed
such notable courses as the Riviera Country Club in Los Angeles (1927) and Ojai Valley Inn and
Country Club in Ojai, California (1925). Mackenzie designed Cypress Point in Monterey, California,
with Robert Hunter (1928); the Royal Melbourne West Course in Australia with Alex Russell (1931);
and the Augusta National in Georgia with Robert Tyre Jones Jr. (1933).

Golf course design has become a lucrative profession in which millions can be earned. Among
the more successful post–World War II architects are Pete Dye, Rees Jones, Tom Fazio, Robert Trent
Jones Jr., Joe Lee, Arthur Hills, Jack Nicklaus, Arnold Palmer, and Dick Wilson, to name a few. Yet
some of the world's best courses—Pebble Beach, Pine Valley, and Oakmont, for example—were
designed by amateurs who had imagination and a feel for the game.

JIMMY DEMARET: GOLF'S HAPPY WARRIOR

Jimmy Demaret was born in Houston, Texas, in 1910. After a stint as a nightclub singer, he joined the PGA Tour. A flashy dresser and a gallery favorite, Demaret was the first three-time Masters winner with victories in 1940, 1947, and 1950. Undefeated in six Ryder Cup matches, Demaret won a total of thirty-one PGA Tour events. A close friend of Ben Hogan, Demaret authored the book, *My Partner, Ben Hogan.* Pictured are Demaret (on the right) and Hogan.

As Al Barkow described in his excellent book *Golf's Golden Grind: The History of the Tour* (1974), Demaret played his shots as follows: "Once over the ball, Demaret kept his feet quite close together and lined them up generally well left of the target. Just before taking the club back he would shove it along the ground until the ball was in the very neck, or shank, of the club. As soon as the club got into that position he took it up. He would cut across the ball from outside to inside his line of flight, and the ball would invariably fly from left to right."

BOBBY LOCKE: SOUTH AFRICA'S FIRST GREAT GOLFER

Arthur d'Arcy "Bobby" Locke was the first great golfer to come out of South Africa. Noted for his short game, especially his putting, Locke won seven South African Opens, four British Opens (1949, 1950, 1952, 1957), and several other international events. He received limited recognition in the United States because he played in relatively few events there compared to his world golfing activities. During his time he was considered a slow player because it took him $3\frac{1}{4}$ hours to finish a round—about $2\frac{1}{2}$ hours faster than PGA Tour professionals today.

Locke believed that his type of swing was a natural swing and that those of American competitors tended to be manufactured. This manufactured swing, he believed, required constant practice and strict concentration to keep in the groove. Locke also felt that American pros overpracticed . He feared that if he practiced too much, he would leave his best shots on the range. Locke was a pleasure for galleries to watch. As the noted golf writer Herbert Warren Wind observed, modern "Golf stars were much more temperamental than opera singers, racehorses and even tennis players. And then along came Locke, recalling not only in his knickers and his swing but in his deportment an earlier era when golf was a friendly game and not a dry run for Purgatory."

CELEBRITY GOLF

Many national leaders and celebrities, including U.S. presidents, have loved and played golf. But few have popularized golf as much as Dwight D. Eisenhower. An all-around athlete at West Point, Eisenhower did not take up golf until years later when he was posted in the Washington, D.C., area. As U.S. president (1952–1960), he had a practice bunker and green installed on the White House grounds. He was a great friend of Bobby Jones, Arnold Palmer, and celebrity golfers such as the comedian Bob Hope. He had a cottage at Augusta National; the trophy for the World Amateur Team Championship was named for him in 1958. Ike sometimes scored in the mid-80s and was noted for his punch shots to the green.

THE GOLF CART

Quaint club names like *niblick* have given way to numbered irons and, since World War II, televised golf and affordable golf equipment have led to unprecedented golf industry expansion and participation. The caddie pull cart and automatic gas- and electric-powered carts were developed to compensate for the caddie shortage after World War II relative to the growing number of golfers. It is estimated that there were slightly over three million golfers in the United States playing on approximately five thousand golf courses in 1950. By 1996 there were more than twenty-five million American golfers and over fifteen thousand courses. In the old days it was de rigueur to play in the rain without benefit of shelter (such as a roofed modernized golf cart) or waterproof gear. Pictured here is Ben Hogan riding an early-model golf cart—notice the hand brake on the handle bar!

PEBBLE BEACH GOLF LINKS: AN AMERICAN GOLF MECCA

Pebble Beach Golf Links, perched along the cliffs of the Pacific Ocean on the Monterey Peninsula, represents golf's manifest destiny in the continental United States. Designed by Jack Neville, with Douglas Grant as a consultant, the 6,832-yard layout opened in 1919. One of the most famous shots here was Tom Watson's final-round chip-in from the rough on the par-3 seventeenth in the 1982 U.S. Open. Watson came from behind to edge Jack Nicklaus by 2 strokes in that event.

Pebble Beach, with eight holes scenically strung along the ocean, became world famous after becoming the site of nationally televised events, most notably the Bing Crosby Professional-Amateur (now the AT&T Pebble Beach National Pro-Am). That tournament originated at Rancho Santa Fe in San Diego in 1937 and was moved to the Monterey Peninsula in 1947.

Palmer, Nicklaus and Player: The International Golf Boom

TELEVISION AND THE TOUR

The success of the post–World War II Tours was spurred by network television fees, which enabled purses to grow geometrically. Stars such as Arnold Palmer and Nancy Lopez helped to increase the popularity of golf, as did rivalries such as those among The Big Three: Jack Nicklaus, Arnold Palmer, and Gary Player. The proliferation of celebrity or sponsored golf events like the Bob Hope Chrysler Classic, the Nabisco Dinah Shore, and the AT&T Pebble Beach National Pro-Am added to the popularity and financial success of the Tours. The addition of post-Tour season made-for-television events such as The Skins Game added year-round coverage to the game.

The late Dinah Shore (left), shown here with Kathy Whitworth and David Foster, (then CEO of Colgate-Palmolive) was elected an honorary member of the LPGA Hall of Fame in 1994 because of her long-time support for women's golf. Other honorary LPGA members include Kathryn Crosby, Grace Fippinger, Betty Ford, Dolores Hope, Dina Merrill, and Mousie Powell. The Nabisco Dinah Shore became the fourth LPGA major in 1983; the others are the U.S. Open, Du Maurier Classic, and McDonald's LPGA Championship. The Titleholders, last played in 1972, and the Western Open, last played in 1967, used to be major tournaments.

ANNE QUAST SANDER: ONE OF GOLF'S GREAT AMATEURS

Anne Quast Sander won the U.S. Women's Amateur three times (1958, 1961, 1963); the Western Women's Amateur twice (1958, 1961); the USGA Senior Women's Amateur four times (1987, 1989, 1990, 1993); and many other events. Carolyn Cudone holds the record for USGA Senior Women's Amateur titles, with five.

Pictured here is Anne Quast Sander playing in the 1967 Women's Open.

MICKEY WRIGHT: AN LPGA CHAMPION WITH A TEXTBOOK SWING

Though second to Kathy Whitworth in all-time LPGA Tour wins with eighty-two, Mickey Wright is considered by many to be the best lady golfer ever. Born in San Diego in 1935, Wright began playing golf at age twelve and won the 1952 U.S. Girls' Junior four years later. She joined the LPGA Tour in 1955 after attending Stanford University. Seventy-nine of her Tour victories were achieved in a ten-year span from 1959 to 1968, an incredible 7.9-victories-per-year average. She won thirteen majors: four LPGA Championships (1958, 1960, 1961, 1963); four U.S. Opens (1958, 1959, 1961, 1964); two Titleholders (1961, 1962); and three Western Opens (1962, 1963, 1966). She was voted the Associated Press Woman Athlete of the Year in 1963 and 1964.

Wright was said to have a perfect golf swing. She took her early lessons from Harry Pressler, the professional at the San Gabriel Country Club near Los Angeles. Fascinated by the theory of the golf swing, Wright followed these maxims from Pressler: 1. At the start of the downswing, the weight should begin moving across the right foot to the left foot; 2. on the downswing, also, the right elbow should be tucked close in front of the right hip; 3. as the hands move toward the ball, the wrists should remain cocked as long as possible. Wright entered the LPGA Hall of Fame in 1964. She stopped playing regularly on the Tour in 1969 for a variety of reasons, including foot problems, adverse reaction to sunlight, and a fear of flying.

KATHY WHITWORTH: WINNER OF A RECORD EIGHTY-EIGHT LPGA TOURNAMENTS

Kathy Whitworth was born in Monahans, Texas, attended Odessa College, joined the LPGA Tour in 1958, and won a record eighty-eight tournaments in her illustrious career. She was the leading Tour money winner eight times, Player of the Year seven times, and a seven-time winner of the Vare Trophy for best scoring average. She won six majors: the LPGA (1967, 1971, 1975); the Title-holders (1965, 1966); and the Western Open (1967). Whitworth claimed that the keys to her success were her putting and ability to keep the ball in play. Whitworth was inducted into the LPGA Hall of Fame in 1975.

ARNOLD PALMER: THE KING

Arnold Palmer, the son of a golf professional, was born in Latrobe, Pennsylvania, in 1929. He attended Wake Forest University then turned professional in 1954, a time when television put the power and drama of his game in the spotlight. Palmer, a charismatic man of great warmth with the arms of a blacksmith and the heart of a lion, brought power, excitement, and an element of unpredictability to the game. He was a great pressure putter and a streak player who, hitching his pants, could mount a charge against any opponent. This was illustrated in the 1960 U.S. Open, in which Palmer came from 7 strokes behind on the last day to win by 2 shots over the up-and-coming twenty-year-old from Ohio, Jack Nicklaus. Palmer won eight tournaments that year; in his PGA Tour career he has won sixty events. Arnie won four Masters (1958, 1960, 1962, 1964); two British Opens (1961, 1962); and the U.S. Open (1960).

Besides raising the level of both interest in golf and the purses on the PGA Tour, much the way Walter Hagen and others did in an earlier time, Palmer virtually put the PGA Senior Tour on the map when he joined it in 1980. He won ten events on that tour, which has given a profitable second life to many golfers. Palmer became the modern version of the one-man golf conglomerate when he teamed up with super-agent and lawyer Mark McCormack, who helped launch Arnold Palmer Enterprises. In many respects Palmer and McCormack developed the business model for the modern international golfer, who can generate millions of dollars in off-the-course revenue from a variety of product endorsements and other business deals. Palmer has designed numerous golf courses with his partner, Ed Seay; is chairman of The Golf Channel; owns the Bay Hill Club in Orlando, Florida; and has been engaged in numerous other business activities.

JACK NICKLAUS: WINNER OF A RECORD TWENTY MAJOR TOURNAMENTS

Jack Nicklaus was born in Columbus, Ohio, in 1944 and attended Ohio State as did his father before him. From an early age he set his sights on the major tournaments as a benchmark of greatness. He has won a total of seventy PGA Tour victories, second only to Sam Snead. His last Tour win, the 1986 Masters, was perhaps his most dramatic. He eagled the fifteenth, and birdied the sixteenth and seventeenth in the final round to edge Greg Norman and Tom Kite by a stroke. He had won his last major at the age of forty-six. His major victories are two U.S. Amateurs (1959, 1961); six Masters (1963, 1965, 1966, 1972, 1975, 1986); five PGA Championships (1962, 1971, 1973, 1975, 1980); three British Opens (1966, 1970, 1978); and four U.S. Opens (1962, 1967, 1972, 1980). Often in a position to win, Nicklaus finished second a remarkable nineteen times in the four major professional championships. He has played a limited schedule on the Senior PGA Tour since joining it in 1990, and has won the U.S. Senior Open twice (1991, 1993) and the PGA Seniors Championship once (1991).

A long hitter with a high fade, Nicklaus was also a great clutch money putter in big championship events. Like Arnold Palmer, Jack Nicklaus is a protégé of Mark McCormack's International Management Group. Nicklaus is now an independent and has developed a variety of golf-related business interests, including an internationally successful golf course design practice and equipment companies. He has authored numerous books, usually with Ken Bowden, including instructional and autobiographical titles such as *Golf My Way* and *Jack Nicklaus: My Story*.

Pictured here is Jack Nicklaus at age twenty, meeting his idol, Bobby Jones, at the Metropolitan Golf Writers' Association Dinner in New York on January 26, 1960. Jones predicted that Nicklaus would achieve his Grand Slam but Jack never won the four majors in the same year.

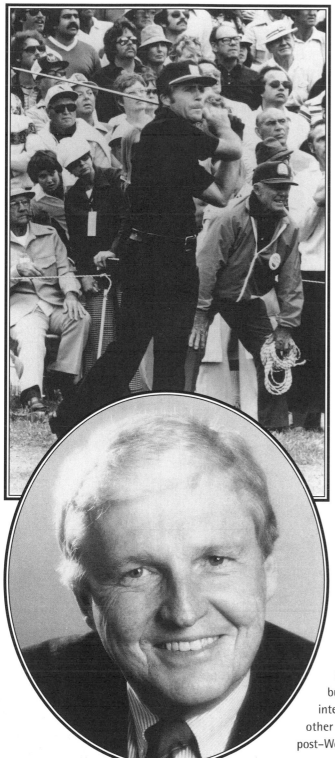

Gary Player: One of the Big Three

Gary Player, born in South Africa in 1935, is the best golfer to have come out of that country. Part of the Big Three with Arnold Palmer and Jack Nicklaus, Player has won over 160 international events including The Masters (1961, 1974); the PGA Championship (1962, 1972); the U.S. Open (1965); and the British Open (1959, 1968, 1974). He has also won a record thirteen South African Opens and several Senior PGA Tour events.

At five feet seven inches and around 140 pounds in his prime, Player adopted a rigorous diet and fitness program to accommodate his international schedule and the demands of competing against longer hitters. In 1997, after winning the Shell Wentworth Senior Masters in Edinburgh, Scotland, Player said, "I'm as fit now as I was thirty years ago and I believe I'll still be winning the big tournaments when I'm seventy." After a victory at Sunningdale in 1958, Player dedicated himself to competing on the American Tour. He is one of the first international golfers to make a strong impact on the PGA Tour.

Mark McCormack: Golf's Super-Agent

Mark McCormack was not the first golf agent, but he has proved the most effective. A native of Chicago and a Cleveland-based attorney, McCormack signed Arnold Palmer as his first major golf client. McCormack's International Management Group (IMG) has subsequently managed Jack Nicklaus, Gary Player, Raymond Floyd, Nancy Lopez, Nick Faldo, Laura Davies, Betsy King, and Tiger Woods, to name a few. IMG has evolved into a sports and entertainment empire with many nongolf clients. McCormack has taken modern legal and business principles and applied them to the happy confluence of international marketing, endorsements, advertising, licensing, and other opportunities brought about by superstars, television, the post–World War II economic boom, and the popularity of the game.

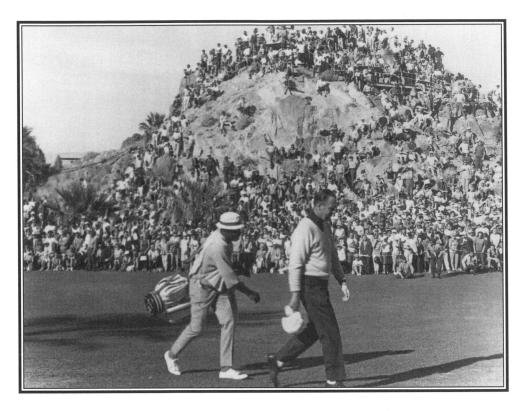

BILLY CASPER: GOLF'S QUIET SUPERSTAR

Billy Casper, a native of San Diego, is often overlooked when citing great golfers of the post–World War II era. He is sixth on the all-time PGA Tour winners list with fifty-one victories, behind Snead, Nicklaus, Hogan, Palmer, and Nelson. Casper won two U.S. Opens (1959, 1966) and the 1970 Masters. He also won the Vardon Trophy for low scoring average five times (1960, 1963, 1965, 1966, 1968) and was a seven-time member of the Ryder Cup team.

Casper's 1966 U.S. Open victory at the Olympic Club in San Francisco is remembered as Arnold Palmer's loss, even though Casper played superb golf in the heat of battle. He came from 7 shots behind with nine holes left, on which he shot a 32 to force a playoff with Palmer. He closed Palmer out 69 to 73 in the playoff. Palmer, then thirty-six years of age, never won another major tournament.

Pictured here is Casper and his caddie on the final hole of the Bob Hope Desert Classic at Indian Wells in 1969.

PETER THOMSON: WINNER OF FIVE BRITISH OPENS

Peter Thomson, one of Australia's greatest golfers, won five British Opens (1954, 1955, 1956, 1958, 1965) and several other international events. He tended to be more successful with the then smaller British ball on fast courses. Because of his limited success on the U.S. Tour, Thomson was never given the recognition he deserved. His disciplined, rhythmic swing held up as he grew older and he found some success on the U.S. Senior Tour. Thomson was also known for his newspaper commentary and television work, as well as his administrative activities for the Australian PGA. Thomson, primarily with Mike Wolveridge, also designed and remodeled several golf courses throughout the world. Here Thomson displays the British Open cup he won at Saint Andrews in 1955.

CHI CHI RODRIGUEZ: GOLF'S HAPPY WARRIOR

Juan "Chi Chi" Rodriguez, the ebullient native of Rio Piedras, Puerto Rico, is one of those players who, after a workmanlike eight-win PGA Tour career, received a second life on the Senior Tour, which he joined in 1985. Since then Chi Chi has won twenty-two Senior Tour events and over five million dollars. He has also raised over two million dollars for his Chi Chi Rodriguez Foundation, which supports junior golf and other worthy causes. Here Chi Chi is pictured with New York Yankee Hall of Famer Mickey Mantle.

REES JONES

Rees Jones, who with his brother Robert Trent Jones, Jr., carries on the Jones architectural tradition set by his father, Robert Trent Jones (opposite).

GOLF GADGETS: IN SEARCH OF THE PERFECT SWING

Over the years numerous practice aids have been developed to cure golfer's sway, flying elbow, and other maladies of the game.

ROBERT TRENT JONES, SR.: THE DEAN OF AMERICAN GOLF COURSE ARCHITECTS

Robert Trent Jones Sr. is the dean of post–World War II American golf course architecture. A native of Lancashire, England, he moved with his parents to the United States in 1911, settled in Rochester, New York, became a scratch golfer, then went to Cornell University and took a collection of courses in engineering, agronomy, and landscape architecture that later became the prototype for a curriculum in golf course architecture. He left school in 1930 and formed a partnership with Stanley Thompson, the noted Canadian golf course architect. Jones has designed or remodeled well over five hundred golf courses worldwide. These range from Royal Dar es Salaam in Morocco to the Robert Trent Jones Trail of Golf, the largest public golf course project ever undertaken, in Alabama. Like other noteworthy golf course architects before him, such as Harry S. Colt, C. H. Alison, Donald Ross, and Alister Mackenzie, Jones became an international golf designer. He benefited from modern trans-portation and communications, enabling him to handle many projects simultaneously. His sons Rees and Robert Jr., after serv-ing an apprenticeship with their father, have become outstanding golf course designers in their own right.

DEANE BEMAN: PGA COMMISSIONER

It is sometimes easy to overlook the fact that Deane Beman, born in 1938, was an excellent amateur golfer who won the British Amateur (1959) and two U.S. Amateurs (1960, 1963) before joining the PGA Tour. Beman succeeded Joseph C. Dey Jr. as commissioner of the PGA Tour in 1974. During his twenty-year tenure he was instrumental in developing Tournament Players Clubs, stadiumlike settings for televised golf; the modern Senior Tour (1980); and the Nike Tour, a minor-league circuit for aspiring PGA Tour players (1990). Most notably, Beman ushered the PGA into the modern era of televised golf, agents, multinational marketing, and sponsorship deals. As a result, many professional golfers can earn a comfortable living as long as they keep their Tour card.

The PGA Tour moved to its present headquarters in Ponte Vedra, Florida, in October 1980. This is where the stadium golf concept was initiated with architect Pete Dye's design for TPC Sawgrass, which features large spectator mounds and grass amphitheaters. Since then, over twenty TPC courses have been built to serve as venues for Tour events.

Pictured here is Deane Beman with his first wife and his 1959 British Amateur trophy.

GOLF ON THE MOON

Golf went universal in 1971 when Alan Shepard, a commander of the Apollo 14 mission, hit a golf ball on the moon with a specially constructed club similar to a 6-iron.

JOANNE CARNER: AMATEUR AND PROFESSIONAL CHAMPION

JoAnne Gunderson Carner—better known as "Big Mama," because of her five-foot, seven-inch frame and undisclosed weight—is one of the best golfers to have played the game. Before joining the LPGA Tour in 1970 at the advanced age of thirty, she won the 1956 USGA Girls' Junior and five U.S. Amateur titles; she also played on four Curtis Cup teams. She has since won forty-two LPGA events and was inducted into its Hall of Fame in 1982. She is the only woman to have won the USGA Girls' Junior, U.S. Women's Amateur, and U.S. Women's Open titles.

Carner had tremendous leg drive and a short backswing as an amateur. She could hit her drives over 260 yards—intimidating to many opponents. One of her more memorable amateur matches was against the French phenomenon Catherine Lacoste at the U.S. Women's Amateur in 1968. The previous year Lacoste, at age twenty-two, stunned the golf world by becoming the first amateur, the youngest golfer, and the first foreigner to win the U.S. Women's Open. Carner was paired against Lacoste in the semifinals of the 1968 Amateur at the Birmingham Country Club in Michigan. The match was even after eleven holes, but JoAnne fired par and three consecutive birdies to close out the match 4 and 3.

NANCY LOPEZ: POPULAR HALL OF FAMER

Born in California in 1957, Nancy Lopez was twelve years old when she won the New Mexico Women's Amateur. Then she won several more amateur titles, including the USGA Junior Girls' Championship (1972, 1974) and the AIAW Championship in 1976, when she was an All-American golfer at Tulsa University in Oklahoma. In 1976, she was named to the Curtis Cup team and the Women's World Amateur team. Lopez turned professional in 1977 and in 1978 won nine tournaments, including an LPGA record-setting five in a row. A winner of forty-eight LPGA tournaments, Nancy Lopez became the eleventh player inducted into the LPGA Hall of Fame (1987). A mother of three, Nancy Lopez brings a sparkling smile and congenial personality to the Tour.

Rhonda Glenn, in her book *The Illustrated History of Women's Golf* (1991) made these observations about Nancy Lopez: "People loved her, but not for her manner and appearance alone—Nancy was a winner. Her poise under pressure was one of her greatest assets. Her swing was unorthodox. She addressed the ball with her hands set low, then raised them oddly as she took the club back. But from the top of the backswing, through the ball, to her finish, she was in perfect position. She hit the ball a long way with her irons, and her driving distance came from a low draw that produced overspin and gave her a lot of roll. She wasn't really a good putter, she was a great one, especially on slower greens, and such an intense competitor that she made many, many putts when they mattered most."

When she was a child, both Nancy's parents played golf. Because the family had modest means, her mother gave up the game so Nancy could play. Her father, Domingo, has remained her lifelong primary instructor and fan.

THE DYES: GOLF'S FOREMOST HUSBAND AND WIFE ARCHITECTURAL TEAM

Pete and Alice Dye are the most formidable male-female design team ever assembled. Alice, an excellent amateur golfer, won seven Indiana Women's Amateur titles, two USGA Senior Women's Amateur Championships, and several other events. Pete, who also competed in major amateur events, won the 1958 Indiana Amateur. Both were successful insurance salespeople in Indiana after having met in Florida, where Alice attended Rollins College and Pete was the coach of her golf team. They started their own design business in 1959, created some low-budget courses in the Midwest, then toured the great courses of Scotland in 1963 and returned to create courses such as Crooked Stick in Indiana in 1964 and Harbour Town in Hilton Head, South Carolina, with Jack Nicklaus, in 1969.

Some of these early efforts featured small greens, undulating fairways, pot bunkers, railroad tie bulkheads, and native grass roughs. Dye designs often reflected a target golf philosophy that required pinpoint accuracy rather than low, bouncing golf shots. An extreme example of this is the island par-3 seventeenth at TPC Sawgrass in Ponte Vedra, Florida. Golf course design efforts in wetlands, deserts, and other locales required environmental zoning clearances, giving further impetus to disrupt of the natural surroundings as little as possible.

Alice, the first woman to become a member of the American Society of Golf Course Architects (1982), takes pride in her positioning of forward tees and assistance with design work. Pete is often on site handling the building of the courses. Many of the Dyes' courses are rated among the best in the world. Among them are Casa de Campo (Teeth of the Dog) in the Dominican Republic (1971); Crooked Stick in Carmel, Indiana (1964); PGA West (Stadium) in La Quinta, California (1986); and The Golf Club in New Albany, Ohio (1967).

TOM WATSON: WINNER OF FIVE BRITISH OPENS

Tom Watson was born in Kansas City, Missouri, graduated from Stanford University, then turned professional in 1971. He has won thirty-three Tour events, including The Masters (1977, 1981) and the U.S. Open (1982). He made his mark with five British Open wins (1975, 1977, 1980, 1982, 1983). From 1977 through 1984 he was one of the best players in the world, winning six PGA Player of the Year awards. He then developed serious putting problems and has won only one PGA Tour tournament since 1987, the Memorial in 1996.

LEE TREVINO: A SELF-MADE CHAMPION

Lee Buck Trevino, a Mexican American from Dallas, grew up in a four-room shack with dirt floors in a hay field near the seventh fairway of the Glen Lakes Country Club. He earned money reselling lost golf balls and started to play with a discarded wooden-shafted 5-iron, which he used to hit apples. Trevino dropped out of school after seventh grade but did not take a serious interest in tournament golf until, as a U.S. Marine in Japan, he made the golf team and played in tournaments in the Far East. Legend has it that once back home, Trevino successfully took on all comers in head-to-head contests in which his only club was a quart-size Dr Pepper soft drink bottle wrapped with adhesive tape.

Like Tom Morris, Walter Hagen, Jack Nicklaus and others before him, Trevino was a money player. He won twenty-seven PGA Tour events, including the U.S. Open (1968, 1971), the PGA Championship (1974, 1984), and the British Open (1971, 1972). When critics observed the frumpy five-foot, seven-inch 180-pound "Merry Mex" during his early Tour years, they gave him little chance of success. As Trevino strode up the sixty-seventh fairway in the 1968 U.S. Open at Oak Hill in Rochester, he had a 4-stroke lead, but commented to an official, "I'm just trying to build up as big a lead as I can so I don't choke."

Trevino has had an outstanding Senior Tour career, winning over twenty-five tournaments and more than six million dollars.

SEVE BALLESTEROS: SPAIN'S BEST GOLFER AND THREE-TIME BRITISH OPEN WINNER

Severiano "Seve" Ballesteros, Spain's best golfer, was born in Pedrena, Santander, in 1957. He learned golf by using a rusty 3-iron head fitted to a shaft whittled from a stick to hit rounded rocks from the nearby beach. He later graduated to the nearby Real Club de Golf de Pedrena, where he caddied. By age thirteen he was a scratch golfer. After turning professional at sixteen, Ballesteros, who spends most of his time competing on the European Tour, won the British Open (1979, 1984, 1988) and The Masters (1980, 1983).

A charismatic, scrambling, streak golfer in the tradition of Arnold Palmer, Ballesteros won his 1979 British Open at Royal Lytham by hitting only two fairways during the final round. On the 347-yard, par-4 sixteenth, he hit his drive into a parking lot—which was not out of bounds—and calmly got up and down from there for his par. An excellent match-play and Ryder Cup competitor, Ballesteros captained the European Ryder Cup team at Valderama, Spain, in 1997.

THE TIGER AND
GOLF TODAY

BERNHARD LANGER: INTERNATIONAL CHAMPION

Bernhard Langer is Germany's greatest player and a major force on the international golf circuit, having won two Masters (1985, 1993) and participated on eight European Ryder Cup teams. He has won many other European Tour events, including the German Open (1981, 1982, 1985, 1986); British PGA (1987); Irish Open (1984, 1987); and Italian Open (1983). Noted for his ongoing battle with the putting yips, Langer now uses an unorthodox grip in which his right hand holds his left forearm. Langer ranks among the top career money winners with over thirteen million dollars in earnings.

NICK FALDO: THREE-TIME MASTERS AND BRITISH OPEN WINNER

Nick Faldo, a strapping six-foot, three-inch, 196-pounder from England, is another international golfer who has made a strong impact on U.S. as well as other golf venues in the modern jet-set golf era. He has won three Masters (1984, 1990, 1996) and three British Opens (1987, 1990, 1992). Faldo has also played on ten Ryder Cup teams and won a number of significant international matches. He led the European Order of Merit money list in 1983 and 1992. Faldo is among the all-time career money winners with earnings in excess of fourteen million dollars. A disciplined, steady player, Faldo was inspired to play golf at age fourteen when he watched Jack Nicklaus compete on television. He has completely rebuilt his swing and fine-tuned it under the watchful eye of the noted golf instructor and swing master David Leadbetter.

GREG NORMAN: THE GREAT WHITE SHARK

A native of Australia nicknamed the Great White Shark, Greg Norman was inspired to take up golf by his mother, also a fine player. Norman turned professional in 1976, at age twenty-one, and won the Australian Westlakes Classic that same year. He is the all-time world money winner, having won fifty-five international events through 1996. Norman won the British Open in 1986 and 1993 but the other majors have escaped him, often in painful ways. The most agonizing was his 1996 loss in The Masters, in which he dropped from 6 strokes ahead at the beginning of the final round to a second-place finish, 5 strokes behind Nick Faldo. Norman shot a 78 on the final day, Faldo a 67.

Because of Norman's great ability but lack of success in the majors, he will be rated just below the top tier of all-time greats. A millionaire many times over, he is a golfing multinational with numerous endorsement deals and a golf course design business. Norman has won the PGA Tour Vardon scoring average title four times (1989, 1990, 1994) and the Arnold Palmer Award as leading money winner three times (1986, 1990, 1995).

JUDY BELL: THE USGA'S FIRST LADY

One hundred two years and over fifty male presidents later, Judy Bell, a former Curtis Cup player, was elected the USGA's first female president in 1996. (Carol Semple Thompson, another outstanding golfer, is the only female member of the organization's sixteen-member Executive Committee.) Bell grew up in Wichita, Kansas, and spent much of her summers in the Colorado mountains. She learned golf at The Broadmoor, near Colorado Springs, and won the first of three Broadmoor Invitational titles in 1957 when she was twenty. Bell was runner-up twice in the National Women's Intercollegiate Championship, once at the University of Wichita and once at the University of Arizona. She was a member of the Curtis Cup team (1960, 1962) and named its captain in 1986. She became a successful businesswoman in retail clothing and restaurants in the Colorado Springs area and, over the years, has served on several USGA committees. Her first major USGA position began in 1981 when she chaired the Women's Committee. In 1986 she became the first woman to serve on the USGA Executive Committee.

TIGER WOODS: THE YOUNGEST MASTERS WINNER

Eldrick "Tiger" Woods, now a PGA professional chasing Bobby Jones, Jack Nicklaus, and other golf immortals, has already made his mark on golf history by winning an unprecedented three consecutive U.S. Amateur Championships (1994, 1995, 1996). A grueling event with a starting field of over three hundred golfers whose USGA handicap indexes must not exceed 3.4, the Amateur requires two days of stroke play and five days of match play to determine the champion.

Woods has proved to have a killer instinct and a flair for dramatic finishes, endearing him to golf galleries, tournament sponsors, and a host of golf marketers. In the 1994 Amateur, Tiger birdied the last two holes at TPC Sawgrass (Stadium Course) to edge Trip Kuehne 2 up. The following year he defeated George "Buddy" Marucci Jr. 2 up at the Newport Country Club in Rhode Island. Woods closed this match by hitting an 8-iron approach shot to within one foot of the last hole for a birdie. In 1996 he dropped an eight-foot putt on the final hole to win a sudden-death overtime victory against Steve Scott at Pumpkin Ridge near Portland, Oregon. Prior to his Amateur Championships, Woods won three consecutive U.S. Junior Amateurs, all of them 1 up.

Woods decided to leave Stanford University after his sophomore year and after he won his third straight Amateur. He won two of the eight professional tournaments he entered in 1996, and stunned the golf world by winning the 1997 Masters by 12 strokes at the age of twenty-one. In 1997 he set the single-season PGA Tour earnings record and appears to be a threat to every significant golf record.

GOLF: SOME MEMORABLE YEARS

ca 1000	St Andrews becomes a golf course
1457	Golf banned in Scotland by King James II
1608	First English golf, Blackheath Common
1743	First golf book, Mathison's The Goff, is published
1744	13 rules established by Honorable Company of Edinburgh Golfers
1754	Society of St Andrews Golfers founded
1845	First gutta-percha ball
1859	Allan Robertson, "first of Champions," dies
1861	Old Tom Morris' first British Open victory
1867	St Andrews Ladies' Club founded
1872	Young Tom Morris wins 4th consecutive British Open
1891	Shinnecock Hills clubhouse constructed
1894	USGA established
1898	Haskell ball patented
1900	Harry Vardon wins US Open
1904	Walter Travis wins British Amateur with Schenectady putter
1907	Dimples appear on golf balls
1913	Greens fee first required at St Andrews
1916	Chick Evans wins US Open, carrying seven clubs
1916	PGA formed

1919	Pebble Beach opens
1920	Alexa Stirling wins her third US Women's Amateur
1926	First Ryder Cup Match
1930	Bobby Jones' "Grand Slam"
1935	Glenna Collett Vare wins record 6th US Women's Amateur
1935	Gene Sarazen hits "The Shot Heard Round the World"
1941	USGA develops "Iron Byron"
1945	Byron Nelson wins eleven consecutive Tour events
1947	Babe Zaharias forced to change from shorts to skirt to compete in British Ladies' Open.
1957	Nancy Lopez born
1959	Jack Nicklaus wins US Amateur
1960	Arnold Palmer wins US Open, defeating up-and-coming Jack Nicklaus
1965	Sam Snead wins his final Tour event
1971	Alan Shepard hits 6-iron on the moon
1983	Tom Watson's fifth British Open victory
1986	Jack Nicklaus wins Masters
1993	Greg Norman wins British Open
1996	Nick Faldo defeats Greg Norman at the Masters
1996	Tiger Woods turns professional

PHOTO CREDITS

Grateful acknowledgement is made to the following for permission to reprint the photographs appearing in this book:

Ralph Miller Golf Library, City of Industry, California: Jacket front and pages 18, 21, 27, 29, 30 (bottom), 32, 33 (bottom), 40, 41, 42, 49, 51, 52, 53, 54, 56, 57, 60, 63 (top), 64, 66 (top), 68, 69, 70, 71, 76, 77, 78, 79, 81, 83, 84, 86, 88, 90, 91 (bottom), 94, 95, 96 (top), 97, 98, 99, 100, 101,102, 103, 104, 105, 107, 108, 109 (bottom), 110, 111, 112, 113 (top), 114, 115, 116 (bottom) 118, 120, 121, 124, 125.

United States Golf Association, Far Hills, New Jersey: pages 23, 28, 30 (top), 31, 33 (top) 35, 36, 37, 44, 47 (top), 55, 61, 62, 63 (bottom), 65, 72, 73, 75, 80, 92, 96 (bottom), 109 (top), 117, 122, 131.

Rhonda Glenn: Jacket back and pages 38, 39, 47 (bottom), 48, 89, 91 (top).

Tufts Archives, Pinehurst, North Carolina: pages 43, 59, 66 (bottom), 47.

Corbis-Bettman Archive, New York City: pages 20, 85, 93, 119, 128.

Joann Dost: page 116 (top).

Jeff Ellis: pages 45, 46.

Mark McCormack: page 113 (bottom).

The Norton Simon Foundation, Pasadena, California, F.1972.35.P: pages 17, 22.

© Lawrence N. Levy/USGA: page 123.

© USGA/John Mummert: pages 129, 130.

© USGA/Robert Walker: pages 127, 132.

INDEX